DREW
BARRYMORE

OVERCOMING ADVERSITY

DREW BARRYMORE

Virginia Aronson

Introduction by James Scott Brady,
Trustee, the Center to Prevent Handgun Violence
Vice Chairman, the Brain Injury Foundation

Chelsea House Publishers

Philadelphia

Frontis: Drew Barrymore takes a break from her busy filming schedule.

CHELSEA HOUSE PUBLISHERS

EDITORIAL DIRECTOR Stephen Reginald
PRODUCTION MANAGER Pamela Loos
MANAGING EDITOR James D. Gallagher
DIRECTOR OF PHOTOGRAPHY Judy L. Hasday
ART DIRECTOR Sara Davis
SENIOR PRODUCTION EDITOR LeeAnne Gelletly

Staff for **Drew Barrymore**
SENIOR EDITOR Therese De Angelis
ASSOCIATE ART DIRECTOR Takeshi Takahashi
DESIGNER 21st Century Publishing and Communications, Inc.
PICTURE RESEARCHER Patricia Burns
COVER DESIGNER Terry Mallon

COVER PHOTO: London Features International (USA) Ltd.

© 2000, 2003 by Chelsea House Publishers,
a subsidiary of Haights Cross Communications. All rights reserved.
Printed and bound in the United States of America.

The Chelsea House World Wide Web address is
http://www.chelseahouse.com

3 5 7 9 8 6 4 2

Library of Congress Cataloging-in-Publication Data

Aronson, Virginia.
Drew Barrymore / Virginia Aronson.
    p.   cm. — (Overcoming adversity)
Filmography: p.
Includes bibliographical references and index.
Summary: A biography of the young star of the movie "E.T." who survived her
troubled early years and has gone on to become a successful actress and movie
producer. ·
ISBN 0-7910-5306-7 (hardcover) — ISBN 0-7910-5307-5 (pbk.)
1. Barrymore, Drew—Juvenile literature. 2. Motion picture actors and actresses—
United States—Biography—Juvenile literature. [1. Barrymore, Drew. 2. Actors
and actresses. 3. Women—Biography.] I. Title. II. Series.
PN2287.B29A88   1999
791.43'028'092—dc21
[B]   99-34256
                                                                  CIP

CONTENTS

On Facing Adversity *James Scott Brady*   7

1   CINDERELLA   11

2   THE ROYAL FAMILY OF HOLLYWOOD   25

3   GROWING UP IN THE PUBLIC EYE   43

4   JUST SAYING YES   55

5   LITTLE GIRL LOST   67

6   LITTLE GIRL FOUND   81

7   EVER AFTER   93

Chronology   106

Filmography   108

Further Reading   110

Appendix   111

Index   115

OVERCOMING ADVERSITY

TIM ALLEN
comedian/performer

MAYA ANGELOU
author

APOLLO 13 MISSION
astronauts

LANCE ARMSTRONG
professional cyclist

DREW BARRYMORE
actress

JAMES BRADY
gun control activist

DREW CAREY
comedian/performer

JIM CARREY
comedian/performer

BILL CLINTON
U.S. president

TOM CRUISE
actor

GAIL DEVERS
Olympian

MOHANDAS K. GANDHI
political and spiritual leader

MICHAEL J. FOX
actor

WHOOPI GOLDBERG
comedian/performer

EKATERINA GORDEEVA
figure skater

SCOTT HAMILTON
figure skater

JEWEL
singer and poet

JAMES EARL JONES
actor

QUINCY JONES
musician and producer

MARIO·LEMIEUX
hockey legend

ABRAHAM LINCOLN
U.S. president

JOHN McCAIN
political leader

WILLIAM PENN
Pennsylvania's founder

JACKIE ROBINSON
baseball legend

ROSEANNE
entertainer

TRIUMPH OF
THE IMAGINATION:
THE STORY OF THE WRITER
J.K. ROWLING
author

MONICA SELES
tennis star

SAMMY SOSA
baseball star

DAVE THOMAS
entrepreneur

SHANIA TWAIN
entertainer

ROBIN WILLIAMS
performer

STEVIE WONDER
entertainer

ON FACING ADVERSITY

James Scott Brady

I GUESS IT'S a long way from a Centralia, Illinois, train yard to the George Washington University Hospital Trauma Unit. My dad was a yardmaster for the old Chicago, Burlington & Quincy Railroad. As a child, I used to get to sit in the engineer's lap and imagine what it was like to drive that train. I guess I always have liked being in the "driver's seat."

Years later, however, my interest turned from driving trains to driving campaigns. In 1979, former Texas governor John Connally hired me as a press secretary in his campaign for the American presidency. We lost the Republican primary to a former Hollywood star named Ronald Reagan. But I managed to jump over to the Reagan campaign. When Reagan was elected in 1980, I was "sitting in the catbird seat," as humorist James Thurber would say—poised to be named presidential press secretary. I held that title throughout the eight years of the Reagan administration. But not without one terrible, extended interruption.

It happened barely two months after the Reagan administration took office. I never even heard the shots. On March 30, 1981, my life went blank in an instant. In an attempt to assassinate President Reagan, John Hinckley Jr. armed himself with a "Saturday night special"—a low-quality, $29 pistol—and shot wildly as our presidential entourage exited a Washington hotel. One of the exploding bullets struck me just above the left eye. It shattered into a couple dozen fragments, some of which penetrated my skull and entered my brain.

The next few months of my life were a nightmare of repeated surgery, broken contact with the outside world, and a variety of medical complications. More than once, I was very close to death.

The next few years were filled with frustrating struggles to function with a paralyzed right side, struggles to speak and communicate.

To people who face and defeat daunting obstacles, "ambition" is not becoming wealthy or famous or winning elections or awards. Words like "ambition" and "achievement" and "success" take on very different meanings. The objective is just to live, to wake up every morning. The goals are not lofty; they are very ordinary.

My own heroes are ordinary folks—but they accomplish extraordinary things because they try. My greatest hero is my wife, Sarah. She's accomplished a lot of things in life, but two stand out. The first has been the way she has cared for me and our son since I was shot. A tremendous tragedy and burden was dropped unexpectedly into her life, totally beyond her control and without justification. She could have given up; instead, she focused her energies on preserving our family and returning our lives to normal as much as possible. Week by week, month by month, year by year, she has not reached for the miraculous, just for the normal. Yet in focusing on the normal, she has helped accomplish the miraculous.

Her other most remarkable accomplishment, to me, has been spearheading the effort to keep guns out of the hands of criminals and children in America. Opponents call her a "gun grabber"; I call her a national hero. And I am not alone.

After a seven-year battle, during which Sarah and I worked tirelessly to educate the public about the need for stronger gun laws, the Brady Bill became law in 1993. It was a victory, achieved in the face of tremendous opposition, that now benefits all Americans. From the time the law took effect through fall 1997, background checks had stopped 173,000 criminals and other high-risk purchasers from buying handguns, and the law has helped to reduce illegal gun trafficking.

Sarah was not pursuing fame, or even recognition. She simply started at one point—when our son, Scott, found a loaded handgun on the seat of a pickup truck and, thinking it was a toy, pointed it at Sarah.

Fortunately, no one was hurt. But seeing a gun nearly bring a second tragedy upon our family, Sarah became determined to do whatever she could to prevent senseless death and injury from guns.

Some people think of Sarah as a powerful political force. To me, she's the person who so many times fed me and helped me dress during my long years of recovery.

Overcoming obstacles is part of life, not just for people who are challenged by disabilities, illnesses, or tragedies, but for all people. No matter what the obstacle—fear, disability, prejudice, grief, or a difficulty that isn't likely to "just go away"—we can all work to make this world a better place.

A happy and healthy Drew Barrymore signs a poster advertising her movie Ever After, *one of three films she made in 1998.*

1

CINDERELLA

That which thy ancestors have bequeathed, earn it again if thou wouldst possess it.

—Goethe

DREW BARRYMORE IS in her mid-twenties, but she seems to have lived a lifetime already. As Gertie, the lovable little sister in Steven Spielberg's 1982 megahit movie *E.T. The Extra-Terrestrial*, Drew Barrymore enchanted millions of moviegoers. Overnight, the seven-year-old girl became famous—America's "apple dumpling," as Drew describes the sickly sweet burden of being a child celebrity.

When she admitted to a serious drug and alcohol addiction at age 13, Drew was back in the limelight, this time as the youngest substance abuser in Hollywood to clean up and tell all. As a sober and hard-working teenager, Drew was typecast, often in stalker or slasher movies, as an oversexed girl in trouble.

With more than 30 movies on her resumé now, Drew is still not completely free of her reputation as a wild child. But she has carefully chosen to play memorable characters in a string of critically acclaimed box-office hits over the last few years, resurrecting her image as a successful movie star with talent and draw.

Unlike other young people who have suffered through unhappy childhoods and troubled teen years, most of Drew Barrymore's mistakes have been embarrassingly, hauntingly public. Intense media scrutiny seems to record her every move. During a deeply personal interview with *Harper's Bazaar* magazine several years ago, Drew responded to an especially intrusive and troubling question by putting her head in her hands and whispering, "Oh, God, I knew you were going to ask me that." After a long pause, she answered the interviewer—fully and honestly—as though it were not only the public's right to know every intimate detail of Drew Barrymore's life, but also her responsibility to share it with us.

Her frank revelations about herself, as a real person and a struggling actress growing up in the public eye, have helped to reveal the false fairy tale of life as a child star, Hollywood icon, and young celebrity. It *sounds* so exciting, fun, and glamorous to be famous at seven years old, a regular at the hottest nightclubs at 11, and partying all night with movie moguls before graduating from junior high school. In reality, however, Drew missed out on having a genuine childhood. Instead, she grew up too fast on the outside while remaining a bewildered child on the inside.

Because she began appearing in films at a very young age, people always ask Drew, "How old are you?" She has lived an accelerated life: she experienced early stardom, alcohol and drug addiction, rehabilitation, a suicide attempt, and recovery, all by the time she was 14. Before she was even 20, Drew was the author of a best-selling autobiography, a cult star of teen stalker flicks, briefly the wife of a 31-year-old bartender, a movie producer and founder of her own film production company, and on the verge of critical recognition as a serious actress with an asking price of $3 million per film role. It is no wonder most people find it hard to believe that Drew Barrymore is so young.

Drew's real-life personality seems to be quite close to the type of character she often plays on the screen: sweet but naughty, childlike but mature, a sexy "apple dumpling." She is as effervescent as the little girl in *E.T.*, as campy as the high school seductress in *Poison Ivy*, as romantic as the good-hearted waitress in *The Wedding Singer,* and as powerful a woman as the feminist princess in *Ever After*. "I don't feel any awkwardness or bitterness toward my life," Drew told *US* magazine in 1998, "and I really like playing characters who feel that way. Who aren't *burdened* by what's existed in their past. And know how to make their pain into their strength."

"I understand there are inevitable things that we have to go through: heartbreak, family problems," Drew continued. "I don't feel like some quixotic idiot who says, 'We don't have to feel pain.' No!" Drew snapped her fingers in emphasis. "Let's *feel* it [snap], let's get down *in* it [snap], let's make it *work* for ourselves. But I want us all to be able to get past it. . . . I believe that you can be the person that you dream of being."

In her autobiography, *Little Girl Lost*, Drew describes a childhood in which she was world famous and publicly adored by movie fans, yet felt unloved, ugly, and worthless. "[S]tardom has always been a role which I've never really accepted. It's never seemed real, like anything I could identify, and yet fame is something that has to be dealt with. I've always grappled with the clash of image versus reality," the author revealed at age 14, writing her book as part of a therapy program to recover from drug addiction. "The public saw me as Drew Barrymore, movie star, while I viewed myself quite differently—as a sad, lonely, and unattractive girl with not much to her advantage. Fame changed everything so suddenly," Drew wrote. "Virtually overnight, everybody knew me, and yet nobody knew me. I mean the *real* me. From early on I was always this remote, dreamy little girl who loved escaping reality by acting in movies. . . . Without work,

Drew poses with costar Adam Sandler next to a mock wedding cake during a promotion for the 1998 movie The Wedding Singer. *Drew's turn as a good-hearted waitress in the film was a departure from many of her previous on-screen roles, in which she portrayed "bad" girls in trouble.*

I believed, I was nothing. I was horribly insecure. It wasn't what anyone imagined me, Drew Barrymore, the celebrated actress and heir to the great Barrymore legacy, to be like."

The only child of a single mother, Ildyko Jaid Mako, who worked many hours as a waitress and occasionally as an actress, Drew was raised by a succession of baby-sitters.

She rarely saw her father, John Barrymore Jr. Her overnight fame at a young age made life very difficult. "It made people think I was someone who I wasn't. I'd walk into a restaurant or some room where there were other kids and sense that everyone was looking at me, thinking, 'I'm sure she's the biggest snob or brat on Earth,'" Drew recalls. "But I wasn't. I was this frail little thing who wanted to shout, 'Hey, I didn't want to be famous. I just want to be loved. I'm scared. I don't know how to deal with this.'"

Without the parental support she needed to adjust to her celebrity status, Drew quickly became a victim of her early success. "I was riddled by insecurity," Drew recalls, "always fearing that people wouldn't like me. 'How could they?' I thought. 'My father hates me. My mother likes me only for the money I earn. And I know for damn sure that I'm nothing but a worthless piece of flesh.'"

Despite her troubles, Drew does not blame Hollywood for her addiction problems. In fact, she feels that it was when she was between projects, waiting for a new script to come in and worrying that no one would offer her another film project, that she began drinking alcohol and abusing other drugs. "Without the ego-boost of work, I got into trouble with liquor and drugs by trying to run from everything," she admits. "Or to numb it. I was the party girl on the run. If I was high, I thought, everything was fine." The only time she would not use alcohol or other drugs, Drew says, was when she was working. "If anything, work was my saving grace, the one tangible thing I could always rely on to boost my sagging self-esteem and confidence," Drew explains.

For Drew, one of the obstacles to accepting herself was the fact that she was a chubby child, and she retained a layer of baby fat until her teens (as many girls do). Although this is perfectly normal, Drew's cute figure appeared much heavier on-screen. As a result, fellow classmates, perhaps envious of her fame and success, made fun of Drew's physical appearance.

In the make-believe world of Hollywood movie sets, Drew was treated as a professional, praised for her talents, and nurtured by a wide array of substitute parents— including director Steven Spielberg, actors Jeff Bridges and Ryan O'Neal, and Stephen King, the author of the best-selling horror tales *Firestarter* and *Cat's Eye*, which were made into films in which young Drew starred. She eventually preferred the company of older people— adults and teens who were film professionals like her. Through her acting, Drew managed to create an "ideal Drew" and the ideal family that she dreamed of and desperately needed.

"I started smoking cigarettes when I was nine and a half," Drew reveals in *Little Girl Lost*. "I was smoking constantly, going out and doing everything I could do to be bad. It wasn't long before I began thinking, 'Well, if I smoke cigarettes, I can drink.' It was an easy step, one that I didn't take alone." When Drew was almost 10, she began to drink alcohol: a glass or two of champagne at a Hollywood party, a couple of beers at friends' houses. "After a while, though, drinking became the only way I thought I could have fun," Drew remembers. "Only I didn't drink to have fun. I drank to get drunk."

When she was 10 ½ years old, Drew smoked marijuana for the first time while sitting in the back seat of a car driven by her friend's mother, who had offered the drug to the two girls. "I was shocked," says Drew. "But she had a look that seemed to say, 'Isn't it cute, a little girl getting stoned.' Eventually, [using pot] got boring, too, and my addict mind told me, 'Well, if smoking pot is cute, it'll also be cute to get into the heavier stuff, like cocaine.' My usage was gradual. But what I did kept getting worse and worse, and I didn't care what anybody else thought about me."

At age 13, Drew tried cocaine at her school prom. "From that night on," Drew recounts in her autobiography, "I craved [cocaine] all the time. Just thinking about it caused my palms to sweat." Drew used more and more cocaine—to help her lose weight, to pick up her mood,

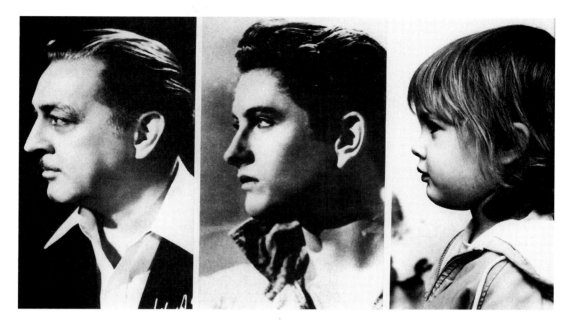

to party all night without sleeping, but mostly to numb the emotional pain she felt almost constantly. "Part of being an addict is involvement in the continuous search for the perfect antidote to pain," says Drew. "For some addicts it's booze. For others it's pills or heroin. You go through them all, [thinking] that something out there is going to make you feel good." With cocaine, Drew believed, she could alleviate her depression without suffering hangovers or having "the munchies." "What I couldn't see," Drew acknowledges, "is that [the drug] eventually makes you go crazy."

Drew is not the first Barrymore to become a Hollywood celebrity and admired actor. Nor is she the first Barrymore to become a substance abuser. The infamous "Barrymore curse," as it has been called, passed down through generations along with a passion for the stage and movie set, is an addictive personality that is ripe for developing alcohol and other drug problems.

Drew's father, John Barrymore Jr., was an up-and-coming young actor who failed in Hollywood and in

Drew Barrymore inherited a legacy of fame before she ever stepped onto a movie set. When she was just four years old, newspapers published her photo beside those of her father, John Barrymore Jr. (center) and her grandfather, John Barrymore (left), who was known in Hollywood as the Great Profile.

life largely because of his addictions. He has been homeless and unemployed for decades. Drew's grandfather, the legendary John Barrymore, was one of the most acclaimed actors of his day, both on the stage and in films, but he suffered the debilitating effects of a lifetime of alcoholism. When he died at age 60, he had only a few cents in his pocket, four ex-wives, and a fatal self-image of complete failure. He saw himself only as a washed-up ham actor, instead of the truly gifted genius he had once been.

Drew's Aunt Diana, John Barrymore's daughter, was another victim of alcohol abuse. She enjoyed a brief period of success as an actress, and she recounted her self-destructive lifestyle in the 1957 memoir *Too Much, Too Soon,* before she died at 38 years old from alcohol-related causes. Drew's great-aunt, Ethel Barrymore, a Broadway star known as "The First Lady of the American Stage," also battled an addiction to alcohol that almost ruined her career. Lionel Barrymore, Drew's great-uncle, won roles in nearly 200 films after achieving notable success in the theater. He was an accomplished artist and composer—and he was also a morphine and cocaine addict.

The Barrymore family story has become part of Hollywood folklore and has been the subject of numerous books, plays, and movies. The name "Barrymore" epitomizes an acting tradition that can be traced back to the traveling performers of Shakespeare's time. From generation to generation, a genius for acting and a tendency to self-destruct have been handed down like a genetic scepter. But Drew aims to be the last in a long line of Barrymore flameouts. As she states simply and powerfully in the final page of her autobiography, "My goals are simple: to stay sober and live a good life."

These days, Drew describes herself as "subdued and mellow," but she is anything but boring. She has sobered up and re-established herself as a viable actress. In her

varied movie roles and in her personal life, she has bloomed. "If you're going to be alive and on this planet," Drew philosophized in *Biography* magazine in 1998, "you have to . . . suck the marrow out of every day and get the most out of it. Absolutely."

With her film career now at full tilt, Drew definitely gets all she can out of life at the brightly colored offices of her West Hollywood film production company, Flower Films, which she established in 1994 with her partner, Nancy Juvonen. In only three years, the two women landed a two-movie deal with the major studio Fox

Known for her warmth and approachability, Drew is often surrounded by fans during public appearances, such as this one at Chicago's Planet Hollywood restaurant in March 1998. "She's so smart and funny and ready to laugh, she has a way of making you forget all the [negative] stuff you may have heard or read [about her]," says former boyfriend Luke Wilson.

2000, amassed a staff of five, and put a handful of their projects into development. Their first film, *Never Been Kissed*, features Drew as a journalist and former geek who goes undercover at her former high school to write a story, but gets caught up in the popularity game all over again. "Three years, that's record time," points out Fox executive vice president Kevin McCormick about Flower Films' quick success. "The deal works because Drew knows the audience she wants to reach."

She also knows what she wants in a romantic partner, and believes that she will someday find her prince. Drew has kissed quite a few frogs during her quest, suffering the humiliation and disappointment of a 51-day marriage, as well as a broken engagement to *Beverly Hills 90210* star Jamie Walters. She has dated a number of actors, and she fell in—and out of—love with Eric Erlandson, the guitarist with Courtney Love's band, Hole.

"I would like to be the most wonderful girlfriend that ever lived," Drew has stated. In 1998, she broke up with 27-year-old actor Luke Wilson, her boyfriend since 1996. But Drew was a devoted and determined companion. While they were together, she claimed, "Hands down, everything I do, I think about how it affects him." Wilson, who appeared in *Bottle Rocket, Telling Lies in America*, and *Home Fries,* is regarded in Hollywood as a "nice guy" who was good for Drew. "She makes so much of an effort in her dealings with people," he said in a November 1998 interview. "She's so smart and funny and ready to laugh, she has a way of making you forget all the stuff you may have heard or read [about her]."

Drew is often compared to pop singer Madonna because she is bold about her body and because she also has an amazing way of reinventing herself. When she was only seven, she was showcased in *People* magazine as a style maven, a trendsetter in fashion. In 1998, she made the cover of *People* for the annual Best Dressed issue. Drew has paraded for photographers in little-girl

The outrageously free-spirited Drew dances on the desk of late-night talk show host David Letterman in 1995. "If you're going to be alive and on this planet," the actress has said, "you have to . . . suck the marrow out of every day and get the most out of it."

party dresses, leather jackets and cowboy boots, lots of makeup or none at all, tattoos that come off and tattoos that do not, designer gowns, and even her birthday suit— all complemented by that beautiful, infectious Barrymore smile.

Drew Barrymore has millions of fans and dozens of

websites devoted to her. Friends, former costars, and directors rave about her. She's a philanthropist, a strict vegetarian, and an avid advocate of animal rights. She's a hippie—an optimist who wears daisies in her hair and believes that deep inside, all people are good. "She is one of the very few people I know who has a sincere and self-motivated desire to give energy back to other people," says Edward Norton, the actor who played Drew's fiancé in the Woody Allen film *Everyone Says I Love You*.

Drew Barrymore is nice to people, and she is approachable. On the street, fans will often rush up and invite her to hear their bands or to meet their parents. Once, when Drew stopped at a McDonald's in New Jersey, a worker recognized her and began to cry from joy and excitement. Drew cried, too.

Drew can be outrageous when she wants to have fun, but she no longer looks for excitement in substance abuse. These days, the only thing Drew is addicted to is living that "good life" she talks about. A number of Drew's friends from her drug-using days are dead or still addicted, and many have been in and out of rehab. "And they find this glamour in self-sabotage—it confuses me to no end," she says. "I don't see the glory in it, I just see the sadness."

"I believe in fate and destiny and karma," Drew told *Premiere* magazine in 1998. "I believe in God. I believe in Buddha, Allah, the Druids." One or more of the deities she has faith in must be on her side, because Drew seems to have created for herself a happy ending to the fractured fairy tale that is the "Barrymore curse."

Joel Schumacher, who directed her in *Batman Forever*, believes that she is an important example of how child actors can be successful without destroying themselves. "The industry needs someone like Drew. She is proof that this industry doesn't kill everybody, that it doesn't eat its young. Someone *can* go through the horror of too much, too soon, and really survive."

Drew Barrymore is, in fact, thriving—as an actress who is coming into her own, an addict who has taken control of her demons, and a believer with a lot of heart. At 24, Drew is already a big star, perhaps fated to play out her role as the latest legendary Barrymore.

Maurice and "Georgie" Barrymore, Drew Barrymore's paternal great-grandparents, in a photo taken during the 1870s. Maurice and Georgie both came from families who were well-known in the theater.

2

THE ROYAL FAMILY OF HOLLYWOOD

WHEN PEOPLE TALK about "family values," they probably do not have the Barrymores in mind. The Barrymore heritage is certainly impressive, including world-renowned talent, a larger-than-life public image, and remarkable acting abilities. But there are also the burdens of substance abuse and high expectations that accompany the famous name.

"I take a lot of pride in my family, even though I just know them from watching them on the screen," Drew Barrymore said of her dead ancestors when she was 16 years old. "I mean, I talk to them a lot, which sounds a little weird. Sometimes I know that they can hear me, and I know that they're watching over me, taking care of me." At Mann's Chinese Theater in Hollywood, stars are etched in the sidewalk honoring Drew's grandfather, John Barrymore; her great-aunt, Ethel Barrymore; and her great-uncle, Lionel Barrymore. Whenever she visits the theater, she bends down to kiss the sidewalk imprint of her grandfather's famous profile. "It has nothing

Georgie Barrymore's brother John Drew—the "First Gentleman of the American Stage"— plays the role of Petruchio in a performance of Shakespeare's The Taming of the Shrew.

to do with being star struck," she has explained, "it's the only link I have to them."

When Drew was about eight years old, the famous Hollywood director George Cukor talked to her at great length about her ancestors. Her parents had not informed the youngster about her lineage, and she had never seen any of the hundreds of movies in which her famed relatives had starred. "I think I learned more in those four hours than from anything I've come across since in any book, movie, or story. . . . I was so enthralled with all the things [Cukor] had said that I didn't want anyone to ruin the image he had placed in my head. Later . . . I became more open to what people had to say about them."

What people have to say about the gifted, spirited, and very dysfunctional "royal family" of Hollywood may not be all good, but the story of the Barrymore family is certainly never boring. The name "Barrymore" was invented by Drew's great-grandfather, Herbert Blyth. As Maurice Barrymore, Herbert was one of the theater's most versatile and outrageous personalities. He was married to Georgiana Drew ("Georgie"), one of the foremost comediennes of her time. Maurice and Georgie Barrymore's three children, Lionel (born in 1878), Ethel (born in 1879), and John (born in 1882), were raised by Georgie's mother, Louisa Lane Drew, a child star of the 1830s who later managed the famous Arch Street Theater in Philadelphia for more than 30 years.

Georgie's brother, John Drew, was an esteemed actor, dubbed the "First Gentleman of the American Stage." Georgie and John's father had portrayed Irish and Shakespearean characters onstage. All of the Drews were descendants of traveling actors who performed Shakespeare's plays throughout Europe as early as the 17th century.

Maurice Barrymore was strikingly handsome, and his wife was a lovely blue-eyed blonde. The glamorous couple spent most of their time performing in theaters around the country, far from their three children. John, Ethel, and Lionel lived with their widowed grandmother, whom they called "Mummum." As adults, the three admitted that they had never really known their parents. It was Mummum who provided the children with a home, a sense of security, and exposure to the theater world.

All three siblings also claimed that they never really

wanted to become actors. Growing up during the 1880s and 1890s, Ethel dreamed of becoming a concert pianist, while Lionel and John aspired to be artists. But acting was the family business, and each of the children felt a sense of responsibility. Ethel accepted her special inheritance as early as age 10, when she informed her brothers that they were going to put on a play. "It's about time we were doing something serious in the theater," she stated. Lionel, who was 11, and John, who was 7, complained loudly, but went along with their determined sister.

Maurice was well educated; he loved books and possessed great talent and wit. He was also an irresponsible drinker, a gambler, and a womanizer. In their sporadic visits with their father, young Lionel and John received "valuable" lessons about a wide array of vices. As a female, Ethel was excluded from their adventures in barrooms and men's clubs. She attended a convent school and prided herself on being a "good girl." At 13, she was instructed to accompany her ailing mother on a trip to California, where the normally high-spirited Georgie, who supposedly called her three children "my little shooting stars," suddenly died. Years later, when the children were grown, John was informed that his mother's last words had been, "Oh, my poor kids, whatever will become of them?"

After Georgie died, Mummum put the teenaged Lionel on the stage. He quickly flopped, but remained on the tour as a stagehand. Lionel disliked acting and spent most of his free time sketching. Ethel, also forced by Mummum to join the tour, spent more time playing the piano in the orchestra pit between acts than she did performing onstage. Money was scarce, so she had given up her dream of becoming a professional pianist.

The summer after Georgie died, Maurice married a pretty blonde named Mamie Floyd. A few years later, on a holiday visit to his father's New York apartment, 15-year-old John was seduced by Mamie Floyd. The boy began to drink alcohol, usually to excess. When Mummum died soon after, in 1897, John's feelings of abandonment and desire to numb the pain with alcohol increased.

Ethel was the first of the siblings to earn success onstage when she toured with her uncle, the popular actor John Drew. She was beautiful, passionate, and unaffected. People loved her, on- and offstage. She was engaged to a number of handsome young men, all of whom she disappointed by changing her mind about marrying. Even Winston Churchill, then a young politician, fell madly in love with her. By age 20, Ethel Barrymore was an internationally famous actress.

At 21, Lionel Barrymore was as handsome as his father —and like him, he spent his time drinking and getting involved in drunken brawls. Serious only about his painting, he appeared in character parts onstage, escaping from a trade he disliked by using wigs, makeup, and affected voices.

Ethel and Lionel's brother, John, made his acting debut in a play with their father, Maurice. John handled his small role with aplomb. Maurice, however, had begun to show signs of the mental illness that would eventually force 19-year-old John to escort his father to the Pavilion for the Insane at New York's Bellevue Hospital in 1901. Ethel signed the commitment papers after the doctors diagnosed their father as incurably insane from syphilis, a sexually transmitted disease. Maurice died in an asylum four years later, at age 55.

Once Ethel had become a star, the Barrymore name was more famous than ever. When Lionel landed a Broadway role, he was hailed by theater critics as "one of the best leading juveniles on the stage [who] gives every promise of being a far better actor than his father." But Lionel still focused his energies on playing the piano, writing music, and painting.

The press began to acknowledge the siblings as a trio. "The Barrymores, Winning Fame While Their Father Is

Most film stars leave hand- or footprints in Hollywood's "walk of fame." But John Barrymore's famous good looks almost required that he leave an impression of his face in the cement walkway of Grauman's Chinese Theater (now known as Mann's Chinese Theater).

Dying," proclaimed the headlines, while reporters obsessively noted the comings and goings of the trio they called "The Flying Barrymores." During the 1903–1904 theater season, the siblings appeared on Broadway at the same time, in separate plays. As close to royalty as Americans could get, "Broadway's Royal Family of Actors" had become a phenomenon.

The Drew and Barrymore names brought such high expectations that they could become an obstacle for a new actor. Lacking formal training, John was often given roles he was not experienced enough to handle, but like his sister, he was very good at playing himself on the stage. In his case this meant playing a charismatic, charming, and mischievous young man. But John often missed rehearsals, showed up drunk, or tried to seduce the pretty female cast members.

When he behaved, John Barrymore was a superb actor, perhaps the most innately talented of the three siblings. By 1908, the magazine *Vanity Fair* had dubbed him "an irresistibly fascinating matinee idol." He electrified his audiences. Women wanted to love him and men envied him; he seemed so sensitive, reckless, and beautiful. John Barrymore was indeed a shooting star.

When John was 28, he married Katherine Harris, the first of four wives. He soon began to regard the marriage as "a bus accident," however. His sister had married a wealthy ne'er-do-well named Russell Colt, who drank excessively, was unfaithful, and occasionally beat her.

At this time, a new form of mass entertainment was being developed: the motion picture. By 1910, there were 10 million American moviegoers; by 1916, 25 million film enthusiasts were spending $735 million a year at the movies. Because theater tickets were more expensive than movie admissions, stage performances soon became the entertainment choice for the elite or well-to-do. Stage actors also began to realize that there was a great deal of money to be made in the motion picture industry.

Lionel Barrymore launched his prolific film career early on, in part because he had developed a phobia about forgetting his lines onstage. (Since movies had no sound tracks in those days, he did not need to worry about memorizing his part.) Ethel, who was by this time the mother of three children, signed a contract for $10,000— a huge amount in 1914—to play the lead in her first motion picture, *The Nightingale.*

John typically played romantic leads, and movie audiences adored him. Getting him to the movie set, however, proved difficult. When he wasn't at home battling his wife, he could typically be found in one of the bars along

Manhattan's waterfront. Sometimes he would go missing for days at a time, wreaking havoc on the budget of the studio that had hired him.

When John returned to Broadway in 1916 in the acclaimed play *Justice,* he stopped drinking and for the first time devoted himself fully to a role. He then starred in a succession of Broadway hits, most notably *Hamlet,* while he continued to appear in a number of well-received films. His classical profile, which he consciously flaunted onstage and in front of the camera, earned him the nickname the Great Profile. One contemporary critic assessed Barrymore's powerful influence on the acting community by declaring, "The ambition of the average American actor is not to interpret drama or create character, but to be John Barrymore."

Offstage, though, John Barrymore's life was neither great nor worth emulating. He had left his first wife to marry his pregnant lover, Blanche Oelrichs, a wealthy poet who wrote under the pseudonym Michael Strange. Their child, Diana, was born in 1921, but John rarely held the baby and voluntarily waived his rights as her guardian. Blanche tried to force her husband to stop drinking by hiding his whiskey bottles or smashing his champagne magnums. The couple battled constantly, each threatening the other with dramatic half-hearted attempts at suicide.

Ethel had also begun to drink after she divorced her abusive husband and was struggling to support her family on her own. Lionel, too, drank steadily, deserting his devoted first wife to marry an ex-lover of brother John's, the rail-thin actress Irene Fenwick. When Irene became a morphine addict, Lionel joined her, and he eventually developed an expensive cocaine habit as well.

Unlike John, however, Lionel continued to work responsibly and performed professionally for the rest of his life. Eventually, Ethel quietly gave up alcohol on her own. But John Barrymore was pulled deeper and deeper into the ugly maw of alcoholism, black depression, and self-destruction. Worse, he flaunted his excesses as he did his Great Profile.

Despite his personal problems, John was still in demand as an actor. He left Broadway and the New York film industry for Hollywood in 1923. Following the impressive box office success of *Beau Brummel*, his first film for Warner Bros., the studio offered him a three-picture deal at $76,250 a picture. But John displayed his scorn for the film industry by wearing old clothes that reeked of sweat, spewing obscenities in public, and drinking to extremes with his bar buddies. He became "the most cussed and discussed" celebrity in town, accused of vanity, snobbishness, egotism, and selfishness. Yet he starred in a number of successful films and remained in California for the rest of his life.

While filming *The Sea Beast*, a Hollywood version of Herman Melville's classic saga *Moby-Dick*, John fell in love with Dolores Costello, a bit player whom he quickly promoted to his leading lady. Smitten, John privately arranged to have their big love scene shot first, and refused to stop kissing the blonde beauty even after the director yelled "Cut, CUT!" *The Sea Beast* was a huge hit, and Dolores became the third Mrs. John Barrymore soon after John and Blanche were divorced.

Before leaving New York City to live in Los Angeles, John had converted his Greenwich Village apartment into a veritable castle, complete with rustic oak ceiling beams, gilded walls, and a roof garden with fountains and bee-hives. He later referred to it as "a home, the last one really I was ever to know." For his newest wife-in-waiting, Barrymore purchased and refurbished a magnificent "castle" on a hilltop in Beverly Hills, California. The spectacular estate eventually included 16 separate buildings with six swimming pools, a bowling green, a man-made trout pond, a skeet-shooting range, and an elaborate aviary. One window contained a stained-glass image of the lovers in *The Sea Beast*.

John Barrymore and his third wife, actress Dolores Costello, shown here, had two children, Dede and John Jr., before they divorced in 1936. John Jr. later became Drew Barrymore's father.

Dolores and John enjoyed long, leisurely trips on his racing schooner, *Mariner,* and his luxury yacht, *Infanta.* The couple worked on films together until their first child was born. But by the time daughter, Dede (Dolores Ethel), and son, John Jr. (John Blyth), were toddlers, John was deeply in debt and had lost himself once more in a fog of alcohol and physical abuse. He was as much a stranger to his two young children as he was to his oldest child, Diana (his daughter by Blanche Oelrichs).

In 1932, the Flying Barrymores appeared together in a George Cukor film, *Rasputin and the Empress.* Their reunion was hardly intimate, however: Ethel remained aloof, Lionel holed up in his dressing room and played the piano, and John continued drinking heavily, his classic face looking bloated and suddenly aged. By this time, John Barrymore had earned a reputation as a drunk. On-screen, he began to play himself, drinking while filming and looking haggard on camera. The Great Profile had transformed himself into the Big Drunk, and his magnificent performance as a desperate alcoholic actor in the black comedy *Dinner at Eight* (1933) seemed to fix this image in the minds of moviegoers. In one particularly telling scene, a sodden actor named Larry Reynault (played by Barrymore) approaches suicide when his departing manager scolds him:

> You know, you never were an actor. You did have looks. But they're gone now. You don't have to take my word for it. Just look in any mirror. They don't lie. . . . Get a load of yourself! Wait till you start tramping around to the offices looking for a job because you know no agent is gonna handle you. . . . You're through, Reynault. You're through in pictures and plays and vaudeville and radio and everything. You're a corpse and ya don't know it. Go get yourself buried.

We know today that alcoholism is a disease and that some people are genetically predisposed to develop it, but these facts were unknown in the 1930s. Although an alcoholic like comic actor W. C. Fields, who was one of John Barrymore's drinking buddies, might have been viewed at the time as riotously funny, most alcoholics were dismissed as pitiful and disgusting—a deadly fate for any celebrity. Although he did not "go get himself buried" for nearly 10 years after making *Dinner at Eight*, John Barrymore had crossed the invisible line from famous to infamous and had become an object of public scorn.

Dolores tried to help her husband, but she refused to follow his doctor's advice to commit the troubled actor to a psychiatric hospital. "I sometimes think it was my fault that all that happened afterward happened," Dolores once admitted. By 1936, she and John Barrymore were divorced.

John immediately married Elaine Jacobs, an ambitious young student at Hunter College in New York, who took advantage of the sick man to gain money, fame, and connections in Hollywood. Their brief union consisted mainly of highly publicized brawls and public reconciliations. After John filed for divorce, Elaine stated, "You couldn't hate him because he was such an abomination to himself." But, she added, "You can't live with a man like that."

Less than a year after he married Elaine, John Barrymore was forced to declare bankruptcy. He had become nearly unemployable because of his memory lapses— an effect of years of alcohol consumption—and his increasingly bizarre behavior. Only those who chose to exploit the Barrymore name continued to hire him. Over and over, he parodied himself in the role of a washed-up ham actor whose final act is drinking himself to death.

Finally, suffering from cirrhosis of the liver (a disease caused by alcoholism), kidney disease, intestinal problems, and eventually pneumonia, Barrymore became delirious and was hospitalized. He lapsed in and out of consciousness, often joking with his grieving visitors, until his death on May 29, 1942.

All three of Ethel's children, "Sister" (Ethel Barrymore Colt), "Sammy" (Samuel Griswold Colt), and "Jackie" (John Drew Colt), tried acting, but none of them was successful. George Cukor thought Jackie had potential, but the handsome young man lacked discipline and spent most of his time attending parties. Sammy Colt had a few brief film roles but was never serious about acting. Both brothers were heavy drinkers for most of their lives.

Sister became an opera singer and the mother of John Drew Miglietta, Ethel's only grandchild. "I found I could get more jobs on my own if people didn't know who my

parents were," Sister once admitted. As the producer and editor of Plays for Living, she helped to create educational plays on alcoholism, drug abuse, and child care. "Theater shouldn't just be an end in itself," she maintained. "We can get the greatest pleasure from it as a tool to achieve even better things in all fields."

When she was 18 years old, Diana Barrymore, John Barrymore's older daughter, was invited to test for the role of Scarlett O'Hara in David O. Selznick's *Gone with the Wind*. (She did not, of course, get the part.) Despite having little training and experience, young Diana received many other offers from theaters and filmmakers.

Despite their similarities, father and daughter had a strained and distant relationship. Diana was a heavy drinker and good-time girl who led a notoriously hectic

The Flying Barrymores— Lionel, Ethel, and John—pose for a publicity photo during the filming of Rasputin and the Empress *(1932). The film was the only one in which the three Barrymore siblings appeared together.*

nightlife. She often sported bruises and black eyes, and after the death of her third husband, an alcoholic B-movie actor, Diana finally sought treatment. After recovering, Diana penned an autobiography, *Too Much, Too Soon* (1957), but afterwards she returned to chronic drinking, other drug use, and disorderly conduct. At 38 years old, Diana was found dead, lying facedown on her bed, nude, with empty liquor bottles and containers of sedatives nearby. The police concluded, however, that there was no evidence of suicide or foul play.

Dolores Costello, John Barrymore's third wife, isolated her children, Dede and John, from Hollywood and shielded them from their alcoholic father as well. A beautiful young woman, Dede evaded acting offers from Hollywood in favor of marriage and motherhood. But John Barrymore Jr., who actually achieved some success as an actor, eventually fell victim to the Barrymore curse.

At 16, John Jr. received his calling. "I couldn't sleep one night. I went for a long walk. I looked up at the stars for a long time and all of a sudden I knew I had to be an actor," he said. The day before his 17th birthday, John Barrymore Jr. signed a studio contract that paid him $30,000 per picture. Publicity for his first movie was massive, and the headlines were predictable: "Return of the Profile" and "Little Boy Barrymore," they read. "If people don't expect too much of me," the young actor commented at the time, "maybe I'll have a chance to work my way up."

Strikingly handsome, Barrymore exhibited a brooding charisma and innate talent in his early films. After he appeared in a Shakespearean drama, *The Big Night*, in 1952, *Time* magazine proclaimed, "Young Barrymore, in a turbulent, demanding role, convincingly earns his right to his famous name." At the suggestion of his agent, John changed his name to John Drew Barrymore.

In 1958, Barrymore played the sadly prophetic role of a dope pusher in *High School Confidential!*, which he

filmed in the midst of a violent breakup with his first wife, actress Cara Williams. "He was terribly insecure," she later said. "I guess it wasn't all his fault. He felt everyone expected so much of him because of his name, and he just couldn't live up to it." The couple had one child, John Barrymore III.

In the early 1960s, after John Drew Barrymore was arrested for a hit-and-run accident and driving while intoxicated, he was ordered by the court to quit drinking and undergo psychiatric treatment. He bolted for Rome instead, where a cheap moviemaking industry provided him with work, money, and celebrity attention. Offscreen John was wild, zooming around town in his red sports

Diana Barrymore (Drew's aunt) sits next to a table littered with bottles of alcohol and wine glasses in her New York apartment in 1953. Diana later underwent treatment for alcoholism but returned to abusing alcohol and other drugs, and she died at 38 years old.

John Barrymore Jr. as Corporal Dasovik in the long-running television program Rawhide. *Drew is John's third child by his third wife, Ildyko Jaid Mako.*

car and earning headlines for flamboyant courtships and frequent arrests. He married the Italian starlet Gabriella Palazzoli, with whom he had a daughter, Blythe Barrymore, before divorcing and returning to Hollywood in 1964.

For a time Barrymore was successful as a TV star, but then he landed in jail several times for a variety of drug and traffic violations. In place of acting, he began to subscribe to mysticism and substance abuse. Eventually, he decided to become celibate and give up material goods, and he took up residence in a cave in the California desert. His friends called him "Saint John," and he was

often spotted on the streets of Los Angeles, shoeless and
panhandling for drinks. Influenced by his hippie dad, John
Barrymore III also hung out with drug addicts and served
time in jail before straightening himself out and focusing
on an acting career. "Maybe I'll have to change my name,"
he worried.

After her recovery from drug addiction, Drew Barrymore had a different inclination. "I wanted to keep my
family's name going, and that was a pretty difficult thing
to live up to. I felt that people were always expecting that
of me," she said. Drew was John Jr.'s third child from a
brief third marriage to Ildyko Jaid Mako. Having been
born into the Royal Family of Hollywood, Drew experienced the dark side of the Barrymore legacy. Even as a
child, Drew Barrymore was expected not only to be wild,
but also wildly talented.

"I used to sit in my room and wonder if [my drug
abuse] was hereditary," Drew recounted for *Interview*
magazine in 1991. "I'm sure it had something to do with
it, considering that practically every member of my family
was an abuser. . . . but I wanted to be willing to be the one
person who would break the chain."

A veteran at seven years old: in 1982, the same year that the box-office hit E.T. The Extra-Terrestrial *was released, Drew was invited to host an episode of the late-night TV show* Saturday Night Live (SNL). *She is shown here with SNL regular Tim Kazurinsky.*

3

GROWING UP IN
THE PUBLIC EYE

BY THE TIME Drew Blythe Barrymore was born on February 22, 1975, in Culver City, California, her parents had already split up. Her father, John Barrymore Jr. (also known as John Drew Barrymore), was already a troubled drug abuser when Drew's mother, Ildyko Jaid Mako, fell in love with him in the early 1970s.

The only child of divorced parents, Jaid had grown up in Pennsylvania, where she spent an unhappy childhood acting wild and dreaming of becoming a movie star. In Hollywood, she went to numerous auditions and supported herself on the money she made as a waitress. While she was working at a hip Los Angeles music club called the Troubadour, John Drew Barrymore dropped in and the two renewed a friendship that had begun on a movie set years before. They dated, lived together at a friend's house (both were broke), then married and settled down in a small apartment in West Hollywood.

Like the two wives who had preceded her, Jaid believed she could change John's addictive, violent behavior. But she, too, became the

Drew was not yet three years old when she appeared with Cindy Williams in the NBC-TV movie Suddenly, Love.

target of his abusive, drug- and drink-fueled attacks. Unable to deal with the responsibility of parenthood, John raged at his pregnant wife. One night, after he totally lost control, beating and kicking Jaid in the belly, she knew she had to leave him in order to protect her own life and the life of her unborn child.

Jaid brought her newborn daughter home from the

hospital to their own one-bedroom duplex in West Holly-wood. A month later, Jaid went back to work, juggling auditions with her steady job at the Troubadour and rely-ing on baby-sitters to care for Drew. Before long, she moved with her baby across the street into a larger, more expensive two-bedroom apartment. Jaid worked day and night, struggling to support herself and her child and to succeed as an actress.

"I was left with a baby-sitter all the time. What effect that had on me at the time is hard to say," Drew states can-didly in *Little Girl Lost*. "I've been told that I was a very good baby, real easy and good-spirited. Maybe I just wanted whoever was taking care of me to like me."

At 11 months, Drew was totally adorable, a pudgy blonde sweetheart who smiled and laughed a lot. One day her mother took her to an audition for a commercial for Gainesburgers dog food, and Drew was placed on the floor on a large cloth, with a tiny white puppy next to her. When Drew stuck out her hand, the little dog licked her, and then bit her. Surprised, baby Drew looked up at her mother, then glanced around the room at the shocked producers, direc-tors, cameramen, and advertising executives. Then she suddenly started laughing. Everyone clapped, and the beaming baby landed her first acting job.

When she was two and a half years old, Drew earned a small role in a TV movie, *Suddenly, Love* (1978). She played a boy in the film, her golden curls cut short, and she spoke her lines without hesitation. "She understood," Jaid explains in Drew's autobiography. "Somehow, at that age, she understood what [acting] was all about."

The earliest memory Drew has of seeing her father is when he made a drunken visit to their apartment when she was three years old. "I was so excited to see him," Drew recalls. "I was just coming to the age where I noticed that I didn't have a father like everyone else, and I wanted one. I didn't really know what my dad was like, but I learned real fast." John stumbled into the room, tossed Jaid onto the floor, then picked up his little girl and threw her against the wall. After grabbing a bottle of booze and smashing some glasses, he fled. Fortunately, Jaid and Drew were unhurt. Like his own father and grandfather before him, John cast a dark shadow on his children's lives, and his erratic presence confused and deeply affected his impressionable young daughter.

When Drew was four, she announced her lifetime ambition. "Mom, I really want to act," she declared. "I like it so much." Jaid, exhausted from her routine of working, caring for Drew, and trying to achieve her own goals in Hollywood, warned her daughter about the many drawbacks of the acting profession. "Mommy, I know it's too hard. That's why I want to do it," Drew responded resolutely. Taken aback by her daughter's determination and precocious self-confidence, Jaid decided to take Drew's announcement seriously. She informed Drew that they would make an effort to launch her acting career.

"Why did I want to act? How did I know so early?" Drew asks in her autobiography. She continues:

> The answer, I suppose, has always been pretty obvious—at least it has to me. I loved being part of the group. Actually, I didn't just love it, I needed it. That's what drove me to club hopping later on. Being part of that really fun *in* group. As a little kid, I was the girl who didn't think anyone loved her, which only inspired me to try to be accepted even more. When you make a movie, or work on any kind of production, I learned, you become part of a very close group. It's a lot like being in a family, a big extended family. And I loved that.

Drew landed the next three commercials she auditioned for, and then earned a part in her first feature film, *Altered States* (1980), starring William Hurt. "I was shocked," Jaid admits. "I'd gone out on eight thousand interviews for films, and here Drew waltzes in and gets one on her first try."

Three-year-old Drew shares a lighthearted moment with her mother, Jaid, in 1978. Drew claims that even as a toddler, she knew she wanted to act. "When you make a movie, or work on any kind of production, I learned, you become part of a very close group. It's a lot like being in a family, a big extended family. And I loved that," she wrote in her autobiography.

Drew loved being on the set. At home, she kept herself amused by roller-skating, drawing and coloring, playing dress-up, or practicing the dance steps she was learning in her ballet class. She attended preschool and played fun games with her baby-sitters. But she was lonely, and she always felt like she was missing something: a normal family, a normal childhood.

At five, Drew had a small part in another TV movie, *Bogie*, a biographical film about the famous actor Humphrey Bogart. She had developed a very creative imagination and often played "make-believe" while in school or at home with her baby-sitters. When Drew was six, Jaid brought home a movie script, which she read out loud to her daughter as though it were a bedtime story. "I loved it," Drew recalls of her reaction to hearing the tale of *E.T. The Extra-Terrestrial.* "It sounds stupid, like a cliché, but I cried and I laughed and at the end, I got a real warm spot in my heart. I mean, how could you not?" Drew said.

Two weeks earlier, Drew had auditioned for the movie *Poltergeist.* Although she had not been hired, director Steven Spielberg asked Jaid to bring Drew back to audition for another one of his movies, an unusual fable about a sweet alien creature who lands on Earth and is discovered and cared for by a little boy. Spielberg thought Drew had the cute appearance and plucky personality he wanted for the character of Gertie, the boy's younger sister.

Although she was nervous before the audition, Drew dazzled everyone during her interview by sharing entertaining fantasies about playing in a punk rock band. Spielberg was impressed by the six-year-old's creativity and all-American looks. He invited her back for a second interview, this time asking her to improvise various emotions with two other kids, Henry Thomas and Robert MacNaughton, the boys who would play Gertie's older brothers in the film. As her final test, Drew had to scream as loudly as she could. She was a superb shrieker and she landed the part of Gertie.

"Right off, I fell in love with Steven," Drew admits in *Little Girl Lost.* "In many ways he was—and always will be—the dad I never had." During the three months of filming *E.T.*, Spielberg invited Drew to his beach house in Malibu, where they frolicked in the sand, collecting seashells and building castles. On the set, Spielberg gave Drew freedom to use her own ideas and encouraged her to come up with lines she believed Gertie would say. "I felt important and useful," Drew remembers.

The youngster also fell in love with E.T., the funny-looking mechanical creature who supposedly was from another planet. "To me, E.T. was extremely real," Drew recalls. "Yes, I knew he was something Steven Spielberg created, but I actually believed in him. I could touch him, hug him, kiss him. He put his arm around me. From the moment I saw him, E.T. instantly became my best friend." Drew talked to E.T. during lunch breaks on the set; she even wrapped a scarf around his neck "so he wouldn't drool all over himself while he ate lunch," she says. "Part of me knew he wasn't real because of all the wires sticking out of his back, but I still felt I could talk to him. And it was safe because he wouldn't tell anybody what I said."

After filming was completed, Drew cried. She hated to leave her two most important friends, Steven and E.T., and she dreaded returning to her first-grade classroom.

Drew talks with director Steven Spielberg on the set of E.T. The Extra-Terrestrial *in 1982. Barrymore and Spielberg were immediately captivated by one another; today, Drew views Spielberg as a respected father figure.*

As a lonely child on the set of E.T. The Extra-Terrestrial, *Drew instantly fell in love with the mechanical creature that "performed" the film's title role. "From the moment I saw him, E.T. instantly became my best friend," she remembers.*

"I went back to school and I didn't have any friends. Nobody really talked to me," she remembers sadly. She had been tutored on the movie set for nearly four months, and she was paid about $75,000 for her role in *E.T.* In some ways, Drew had already grown up and was very different from other kids her age, but she still felt like a sad little girl, alone and friendless at Fountain Day School and left at home with a parade of baby-sitters.

A few weeks after school let out for the summer, *E.T. The Extra-Terrestrial* premiered in Los Angeles. "There was absolutely no way to prepare for what happened to me—to all of us—from the morning after *E.T.* came out and on," recalls Drew. "For me it was like walking into a thunderstorm without warning or protection."

While *E.T.* opened to rave reviews, Drew stayed at the Universal Sheraton Hotel playing games and telling ghost stories with her film brothers, Henry and Robert. By the time the three children left their hotel room the next morning, they were famous. "Every place we went, we were followed. People asked for autographs. They stared. They knew my name. They wanted to talk to me. They wanted to touch me. They asked me to tell them what E.T. was *really* like. I thought it was insane. I didn't know how to deal with it, and that frightened me," Drew says. Even at seven, Drew knew that her life had suddenly, dramatically changed. "And quite honestly," she admits, "from that day forward, my life was never the same."

Reporters gathered at Drew's home, and a flurry of stories on the "hot tot" appeared in magazines and newspapers all over the world. Drew learned for the first time that she was descended from a long line of acclaimed actors—that she was just the latest Barrymore to become a Hollywood celebrity. Her photograph appeared in *People* magazine, a snub-nosed child's profile next to an old shot of her grandfather, the Great Profile.

"Too much, too soon" could have become Drew's slogan as easily as it was her aunt Diana's. She went on limousine rides and held autograph sessions, photo shoots, and media interviews. And there were "so many parties," Drew groaned at the time. "Sometimes I'm so tired that I wish I could be alone so I could sleep. I LOVE to sleep," the famous youngster declared.

The press warmed to Drew at once, typically portraying her as a bright, energetic, and amusing cherub, if a bit untamed. *Ladies' Home Journal* reported that Drew ran around the elegant Plaza Hotel, randomly pushing elevator buttons and doing cartwheels down the hall, then yelling the well-known movie line into the suite adjoining her mother's: "E.T., phone home!" *People* magazine dubbed her a fashion trendsetter, photographing her wearing a party dress and sucking her thumb. And there were endless comparisons to her ancestors, the famously flamboyant Flying Barrymores.

"At first I didn't really understand what it was all about.

I just knew that I was a young Barrymore, an actor, and that according to what everyone told me, I was supposed to be great," Drew remembers about that time. That same year, a commemorative 20-cent stamp was issued to pay tribute to her ancestors, the three Barrymore siblings, as part of the U.S. Post Office's Performing Arts Series. At a ceremony in New York City honoring the event, Drew remembers wearing a white dress, white tights and shoes, and a long, frilly ribbon in her hair.

Many famous actors were in attendance, including Lillian Gish, who advised the young actress, "If this is your heart's desire and what you really want to do, I hope you do it always. It will be good to you." Those in attendance reminisced about their former colleagues and costars, the Royal Barrymores, and George Cukor asked Drew to stand up so that the crowd could acknowledge the newest generation of the legendary family. "I felt strangely connected to all that heritage," Drew said later, "strangely because it was only through the complete accident of birth and nothing I did. Yet, I felt it, and, I suppose, subconsciously began to assume the role of the latest Barrymore actor, which was a lot to live up to."

In September 1982, Drew returned to Fountain Day School and the routine of a more regular life. She had spent the summer promoting *E.T.* in France, England, Norway, Germany, and Japan. She had appeared on *The Tonight Show* with Johnny Carson and had served as the youngest guest host in the history of *Saturday Night Live*. School, however, felt like a foreign—and threatening—environment. "God, it was so different," Drew recalls in her autobiography. "Everyone looked at me as if I were the Creature from the Black Lagoon. Or some kind of mutant celebrity. I wasn't the same little kid anymore, that much was obvious, and it was a very scary feeling."

The kids teased Drew as though *she* were the alien from another world. "Hey, E.T.," they yelled, "how come you look so funny?" Her massive fame set her apart from the other children, even the ones who were also child actors. Drew began to feel increasingly insecure. Her parents were in the midst of a messy divorce battle, and every time she saw her father he was unstable, angry, and intoxicated. "Hey, Drew. You want to get me an autograph, too?" her inebriated dad asked on one of his infrequent visits. "How 'bout putting it on a check?"

During this troubled time, the precocious seven-year-old realized that she had been lying to herself. She suddenly knew that John Barrymore Jr. was never going to be the kind of father she needed and dreamed about. Angry and disgusted, Drew threw John's cigarettes at him and screamed, "Your goddamn drinking and drug use makes me sick and I want you out of my life!"

Drew would not see her father again for seven years—and by that time, her own drinking and drug use would be making her sick.

"I want to be a star," Drew told People *magazine when she was seven, "because it makes you feel good."* The success of E.T. The Extra-Terrestrial *set the young actress on the path to fame, but before long she became mired in insecurity, drug abuse, and despair.*

4

JUST SAYING YES

AFTER THE SUCCESS of *E.T. The Extra-Terrestrial,* Drew's mother brought home a new movie script. The story appealed to Drew because she could identify so completely with the character she would play.

Irreconcilable Differences tells the sad, sometimes comic story of a nine-year-old girl who legally divorces her self-centered, continually bickering Hollywood parents (played by Ryan O'Neal and Shelley Long). Her lawyer files her case under California's Emancipation of Minors Law, in which an individual under the age of 18 can divorce his or her parents by proving that the change is in the minor's best interest. It is likely that playing the role of plucky Casey Brodsky inspired Drew herself to file for and obtain a legal divorce from her own parents seven years later.

The film was not a critical or commercial success, however, and unlike the family atmosphere of *E.T.,* the people involved in making *Irreconcilable Differences* argued behind the scenes. Drew was disillusioned. The fatherly Ryan O'Neal tried to comfort her between the more difficult takes, but Drew considered quitting the business entirely after the filming ended. After all, acting was supposed to provide her with an escape from real-life problems.

In one prophetic scene, Casey attends a New Year's Eve gala at her divorced father's ostentatious Hollywood mansion. The girl feels awkward and out of place, especially since her screenwriter father ignores her to fawn over his new girlfriend. When a tuxedoed waiter saunters by, Casey grabs two glasses of champagne and guzzles them.

With the money Drew earned from acting, Jaid purchased a house in a pleasant neighborhood in the San Fernando Valley. Drew began attending a new school, a private academy called Westland, where the school term was already in progress. Drew was the "new kid" and a celebrity, and she became a target for negative attention. "There's a huge difference between people you know making fun of you, which is uncomfortable, and a whole bunch of people you've never seen before just staring at you, waiting for you to make a mistake," Drew explains in *Little Girl Lost*. "The one is understandable, the other is downright mean. Kids can be the meanest too."

At home, Drew was annoyed that her mother never dated, that she didn't seem interested in finding another father for Drew and creating a "normal family." She began to resent the fact that her mother spent most of her time reading scripts and discussing Drew's career with agents—especially after Drew's unpleasant experience in *Irreconcilable Differences*. But Drew's enthusiasm returned after her mother found a script that she liked: *Firestarter*, based on a horror story by Stephen King. She landed the lead role in a cast that included veteran actors George C. Scott, Martin Sheen, and Art Carney.

Filmed in North Carolina, *Firestarter* provided Drew with an excellent escape from her difficult home life. Although Jaid rented an old house in the suburbs of Echo Park during the filming, Drew spent most of her time on

the set. She loved the cast, the grueling work, and the scary special effects. Drew also became very fond of King, who later invited her to spend time with his family in Bangor, Maine, where he told ghost stories every night before sending Drew and his own kids off to bed.

In most films, the stars who play lead roles are assigned "doubles" or "stand-ins," other actors who take their place while cameras are adjusted or scenes are mapped out. In North Carolina, eight-year-old Jennifer Ward was Drew's double—and her best friend. Drew and Jennifer became inseparable, both on and off the set. The Wards lived down the street from the house Jaid had rented, so Drew spent all of her free time at Jenny's. She went to church with the Ward family, ate meals at their table, and played with Jenny's little brother, John. "I was part of a family," Drew recounts, "and it gave me a secure and comfortable feeling." When the filming ended and she had to say good-bye, she broke down crying.

Drew Barrymore as Casey Brodsky (left), a nine-year-old who divorces her parents (played by Shelley Long and Ryan O'Neal, right) in Irreconcilable Differences *(1984). In 1990, 15-year-old Drew would divorce her real-life parents, John and Jaid Barrymore.*

While filming Firestarter *(1984), Drew became fast friends with her stand-in, Jennifer Ward, and with Stephen King, the author of the story on which the movie was based. She later claimed that this period was one of the few times when she felt like part of a real family.*

At the wrap party, where cast and crew gather to say their farewells, Drew convinced two older crew members to let her drink some of their champagne. Like the character she played in *Irreconcilable Differences,* she downed two glasses in a few big gulps. "What does passing out mean?" she asked them. The last thing she remembered was the answer: "Falling asleep."

Returning to Los Angeles meant going back to school for Drew, this time to the Country School, another private academy. Once again, the school year was already under way when Drew entered her third-grade class. She hated the school's rules and unfriendly faces, and she turned her energies in another direction—the Los Angeles nightlife. The party scene was exciting and fun, the perfect antidote to the downers of Drew's school and home life. And from the start, she felt as if she belonged to this crowd. "If for no other reason than [that] I was Drew Barrymore, the celebrity, I was part of it," she said. "[I was] some-one. Being in the thick of all those people was like a big security blanket."

While filming *Firestarter*, Drew had been offered a role in another movie based on a Stephen King horror story, *Cat's Eye,* which would also be filmed in North Carolina and with the same crew, including Drew's friend Jenny. The summer after she completed third grade, Drew and her mother returned to the suburban street where the Wards lived, and the two girls immediately resumed their close friendship.

In North Carolina with Jenny, Drew was a normal, happy nine-year-old who knew how to have good, inno-cent fun. On the set, Drew and Jenny enjoyed jumping up and down on an enormous bed, part of the oversized furniture designed for the movie. When an assistant director complained to Drew's mother of the danger involved, Jaid responded curtly, "Yes, I know. But she's been working all morning and needs to play. She's a kid."

At summer's end, the movie wrapped and Drew had to face the inevitable return to Los Angeles. "I cried so hard. I loved Jenny and her family. I loved the life I had there, but I knew it wasn't mine," Drew states in *Little Girl Lost.* Back on the West Coast, Drew resumed the life of a much older person—a party girl who was a part of a nightlife that she was legally too young to be involved in. Before long, her life began to spin out of control.

Firestarter and *Cat's Eye* were not commercial successes, and as a result, Drew began to face rejection at auditions. "It was as if someone had taken all of my dreams and literally spit them back in my face," she recalled years later. At school, she quickly fell behind in her work, and she became the victim of a group of boys who delighted in tormenting her. "Almost daily they hit me with books,

Drew and best friend Jessica Kline attend a Hollywood premiere in 1984.

called me names like fat ass, pig, fatso, and said my nose looked like Porky Pig's." Drew admits, "The worse they treated me, the more I wanted to fit in and the harder I tried. I had suffered enough rejection, I didn't want any more."

Her loneliness and unhappiness began to transform

itself into anger. The normally sweet and good-natured Drew became moody and rebellious. Her classmates' cruelty made her feel even more rejected and abandoned. She ached for the sense of belonging she felt when she was working, and she knew she would never find acceptance at home or with kids her own age.

"Only one situation came close to substituting for work—the clubs and parties my mom and I attended on weekends," Drew recalls. "They were as near to make-believe as a nine-year-old could find. It was Disneyland for adults, only I got to be part of it." Jaid and Drew spent as many as five nights a week at dance clubs, bars, and private parties. "But nothing was ever enough for me," confesses Drew, who received extra attention everywhere she went because she was young and cute.

Jaid and Drew began to argue frequently. The battles escalated into a constant struggle, with Drew raging about her lack of freedom. "I thought the key to happiness was being older," Drew says of her thinking at the time. She continues:

> Twenty-one became my magic number. Adults, I figured, didn't have to answer to anyone, they didn't have to follow rules. My role models were those people I saw at clubs, dressed up, laughing, carrying a drink, staying out till two or three in the morning. They seemed to have all the fun, and I didn't have any. Or at least not enough.

Drew's "role models" were all more than 21 years old. Drew had not yet turned 10.

When she began smoking cigarettes, Drew fully expected to be caught and severely punished by Jaid, who despised the habit. To her surprise, she avoided detection. Drew quickly realized how easy it was to lie to Jaid: "She didn't suspect a thing," she recalls. "That was an eye-opener as well as an invitation to try the same thing some other time."

Although Jaid had established specific rules for Drew to

Wearing make-up and a lacy evening gown, 10-year-old Drew is the guest of honor at a birthday party hosted by Jaid Barrymore. Around this time, Drew says, she began to realize that her mother's rules could easily be sidestepped. "It was becoming clear, I believed, that rules didn't apply to me," she wrote in her autobiography.

live by, it soon became apparent to her that she could get away with practically anything. For example, when she did get caught smoking and Jaid grounded her, the punishment would end with the next party invitation. "It was becoming clear, I believed," Drew writes in *Little Girl Lost*, "that rules didn't apply to me."

Like cigarettes, alcoholic beverages were regarded by Drew as symbols of coolness and maturity, an indication that the user was a member of the "in" crowd. For her, the challenge was to look grown-up at the clubs without getting caught by her mother. At a birthday party for actor Rob Lowe, Drew and a friend spent the night sneaking beer and ogling the young stars, including Emilio Estevez and Demi Moore. Stimulated by the pulsing dance beat and the alcohol she had consumed, Drew began making out with Lowe's stepbrother, who was about 12 years old. They were so young, Drew says, that they weren't even aware of exactly what they were doing. "We were imitating the older people," she explains.

Drew had begun to discover another potential "addiction"—sex—or in this case, attention from an older boy, which seemed to satisfy a constant need for affection. She concedes:

> I was always searching for father figures in older men, particularly the ones I worked with. But kissing boys gave me a way to get closer than I'd ever dreamed. It made me feel so good. I became guy crazy, an addiction in which I used boys to find love, affirmation, and self-worth. I was like that song, "searching for love in all the wrong places."

For Drew's 10th birthday, Jaid organized a surprise party at a popular nightclub in New York City. The bash included plenty of celebrities and Drew was the center of attention. Yet she felt frustrated all night. "To anyone but me, it was a dream party," Drew remembers. "What bummed me out was the fact that I couldn't sneak a drink."

By the time Drew was 11, she was too old to play cute Gertie-type film roles, but too young for teenage parts. Her self-esteem, always shaky but strengthened by her acting career, plummeted. She poured herself into the role of party girl, dressing in miniskirts, high heels, and heavy makeup, and looking like women at least a half-dozen years her senior. At the trendiest nightclubs, which she frequented with Jaid, celebrities like Madonna and Cher sported far more outrageous outfits. Her mother, for some reason, thought that Drew looked "adorable" in her trampy costumes. Not surprisingly, Drew was often approached by older boys, whom she would persuade to purchase drinks for her. She drank heavily, and sometimes she passed out before she even got home.

One night, while driving home from a club, a friend's mother offered her two young passengers a tiny gold pipe of marijuana. Drew immediately added getting stoned to her list of addictive behaviors. She found pot easy to come by—much easier than alcohol for an underage user. She became extremely secretive and evasive about her activities in an effort to hide her drug use from Jaid.

At school, Drew dressed sloppily and earned Cs and Ds. She felt like "the lowliest, homeliest, and dumbest creature at the place," and she used more alcohol and pot in a desperate attempt to temporarily ease her emotional suffering. After a summer in Germany filming a TV movie, *Babes in Toyland,* Drew fell even deeper into the whirlpool of depression, which she tried to "treat" with drugs. But the drug use inevitably brought on more severe depression. Drew felt so bad, she remembers, that she considered suicide. But instead she opted to get high again. "I remember thinking, 'Well, if I'm not going to die and get rid of the bad feelings, then I will drink them away.'"

By this time, Drew had transferred to Cal Prep, another private school. There, she found a group of older kids who accepted her—seniors who smoked cigarettes and got high on pot instead of attending classes. Her friends had cars, and Drew suddenly had the mobility and freedom she had craved for years. Drew says that she was "adopted like a mascot, an advanced teeny bopper" who "knew how to smoke, drink, cuss, and flip off authority with a disrespectful joke."

Drew finally felt like part of a group, and she dared not jeopardize her acceptance by behaving like "a dopey eleven-year-old who tagged along." Instead, she acted as wild as her friends did, attending parties constantly and avoiding her mother as much as possible. She began to view her mother as an enemy, someone who was exploiting her own daughter by "living off the money I earned and going to clubs on the carpet of my fame."

Although she did not realize it, Drew had slipped into the same pattern of behavior exhibited by her father. She stayed out late, avoided her responsibilities, and screamed at Jaid. During one heated argument, Drew slapped her mother's face. She had yet to recognize the truth: like her father, her grandfather, her aunt Diana, and a pathetically long line of other vulnerable Barrymores, she had become an addict. Using drugs had dramatically changed Drew's personality, bringing out dark, self-destructive inner demons—the kind that had destroyed many Barrymores before her.

The 12-year-old actress in a publicity photo for the TV movie Conspiracy of Love. *By this time, Drew had already begun drinking and smoking marijuana; the year after this photo was taken, she would sink even deeper into drug abuse by using cocaine in a mistaken attempt at losing weight.*

5

LITTLE GIRL LOST

ALTHOUGH DREW WAS cast in *See You in the Morning*, a family drama about divorce and remarriage costarring Jeff Bridges and Farrah Fawcett, she had no desire to be in the movie. She hated leaving Los Angeles and her friends to film in New York. She was so worried that she would be unable to drink alcohol and smoke pot while on location that she attempted to get out of her contract. Ignoring the young actress's vehement objections, Jaid and Drew's agent prevailed. Drew cried all the way to the airport and during much of the flight to Manhattan.

In New York, Jaid purchased a two-bedroom condo, and Drew found some older girls to accompany her to the "in" night spots. Because she believed strongly in being professional while on the job, she was careful to limit her nightlife to weekends when she was not on the set. All the same, in *See You in the Morning,* Drew looks gawky and overweight, and seems as glum as the character she portrays. "Cathy" wears braces on her teeth and rarely smiles. She complains to her

The cast of the romantic comedy See You in the Morning: *Drew Barrymore, Macauley Culkin, Jeff Bridges, Alice Krige, Heather Lilly, and Lukas Haas.*

gorgeous mother about her own unattractiveness. Drew herself was turning 13, and she felt ugly and overweight, as many girls (and boys) do at that awkward age.

See You in the Morning was unsuccessful with critics and moviegoers, and Drew, who had not made a hit film since *E.T. The Extra-Terrestrial,* grew pessimistic about her movie career. Jaid lined up a new kind of role for her daughter, however—a stalker movie called *Far from Home,* which was scheduled to begin filming in rural Nevada the following summer. Drew landed the lead part of an innocent teen stranded at a creepy trailer park during a cross-country trip with her divorced dad. She had to strip down to a black bikini in one scene, and fight off a rapist while wearing a wet T-shirt in another.

Drew desperately wanted to lose some weight, and all of her friends seemed to use cocaine, which reportedly helped people stay slim. On the night of her prom, already so drunk and stoned that she could barely walk, she snorted her first lines of cocaine. Overnight, Drew became a cocaine addict. "My mind seemed to have a huge neon sign in it that blinked nonstop: COKE. GET COKE. So I did." And no matter how much cocaine Drew snorted, she always craved more.

One warm June night, Drew drank more than a dozen beers while at a drive-in with her friends. She stumbled through the door of her home and started screaming at her mother, who stared sternly and silently at her intoxicated daughter. Enraged by her mother's cool detachment, Drew indulged in a wild temper tantrum, smashing glasses, vases, and anything else she could reach. "I went from party girl to jerk of the planet," she told *People* magazine six months later. Before shutting herself in her room, Drew grabbed a beer out of the refrigerator.

Jaid telephoned a friend whose daughter had recently undergone treatment at a rehabilitation facility for alcohol and drug abusers. "I walked out to get another beer and was huffing and puffing and swearing at my mother when the front door swung open," Drew remembers. Sobbing with fear in the belief that her mother had called the police to haul her off to jail, Drew collapsed on the couch when she saw the familiar faces of her newly sober friend, Chelsea, and Chelsea's concerned mother.

The three women drove Drew to the same private rehab facility where Chelsea had "cleaned up," the ASAP Family Treatment Center in Van Nuys, California. It wasn't jail, but to Drew it was pretty close. Drew was interviewed and admitted, then shown to a windowless room for a few hours of sleep. In the morning, suffering from a bad case of nerves and a horrible hangover, she met her therapist, Betty Wyman. "What a sad, sad kid," Wyman recalls thinking at the time.

Drew was forced to adapt to a rigid daily schedule: waking up at 7:30 A.M., attending classes from 9:00 to

A tipsy-looking Drew is carried through Los Angeles's Hard Rock Cafe by a security guard. The year after this photo was taken, Drew would enter the ASAP Family Treatment Center to recover from alcohol and other drug abuse.

noon, and then participating in various types of therapy sessions—individual, group, and family meetings—until evening. Lights went out at 10 P.M. She was also expected to adhere to a strict code of behavior, which included punishments for infractions such as being late, cutting in line at mealtime, or "SAOing"—that is, sexually acting out (kissing or any other sexual activity). ASAP's philosophy aimed at bringing young addicts back to health by helping them confront the issues that triggered their addictive behavior. To recover, patients had to acknowledge their dependence on alcohol and other drugs, and they had to try to resolve the problems that led to their substance abuse.

For perhaps the first time in her life, Drew was around a group of kids who were very much like her. Most of the patients undergoing treatment at ASAP had started using alcohol or other drugs as early as she had. Drew's circumstances may have been more public than those of other patients, but her problems with drugs and alcohol were, unfortunately, fairly common.

But Drew strongly resisted becoming involved in the program:

> When I first arrived at the hospital I was extremely stand-offish, the most distant, obstinate person in the entire hospital. People asked me a million questions and I wouldn't answer them. I just sat in the various [therapy] groups, twirling the ends of my hair around my fingers, letting whatever anyone said drift in one ear and out the other. Nor did I participate in any of the [group therapy] discussions. I wasn't going to admit that I had any problems. No way. That meant facing up to everything that I'd been running from.

Drew stayed at ASAP for only 12 days: her mother did not want to break Drew's film contract for *Far from Home*, so she cut short the treatment. Drew had convinced herself that she could not relate to any of the other patients, and whenever she had to introduce herself in the standard manner used by recovery programs—"Hi, I'm Drew. I'm an addict and alcoholic. And I have 12 days of sobriety"—she knew that she was "just mouthing words. Inside, I didn't believe any of that stuff. I was only obeying the rules," she recalled in her autobiography.

The ASAP hospital officials assigned Diane, a "tech" or former patient who had begun working with addicts, to travel to Nevada with Drew and her mother for the filming of *Far from Home*. Diane shared a room with Drew on location in a small town. Drew enjoyed her work and her time with Diane. "If anyone had asked me one month earlier if I could've stayed sober for twelve days in a small town with just three bars and nothing else to do, I would've laughed and said, 'No way,'" Drew confesses in *Little Girl Lost*. Even when the production moved to Carson City, a gambling mecca similar to Las Vegas, Drew remained sober, but she spent all her free time hanging out with the rest of the movie crew in the all-night casinos and bars in town. "When one of my friends would order a drink, I'd stare at it, feeling incredibly anxious, like I wanted to grab the glass and down it," she recalls of that difficult period.

After the two months of filming ended, Drew returned to ASAP. The transition was difficult for the actress, who felt angry about reentering the hospital: "'Where's my fun?' I thought. 'I've been missing all my friends for a long time and I have to come back to this place?'" Drew refused to admit—to herself or anyone else—that she was still an addict, even though she had managed to stay "straight" while away from ASAP. "Even though I had not been drinking or doing drugs, I had still been hanging around with a crowd that did. They call that dry time, not sober time. You sit around the things you're trying to get away from, and your feelings are still very much involved."

Against the advice of hospital officials and therapists, Drew again left the rehab facility to go work, this time after only six days of treatment. Jaid took Drew to New York to audition for a play. By then, Drew had been sober for 76 days, but on the plane heading east, she felt frightened. "I was real afraid of what might happen to me," she remembers.

In New York, Drew resumed her old habit of going out with older friends to nightclubs. One night in a ladies room, after her friends repeatedly offered her some of the cocaine they were using, Drew began to cry. "I felt really, really sad, overcome by sadness," she says. "I looked at my watch and blew it right there. . . . I did a line. And then another."

Drew had felt understandably proud of her commitment to staying sober. Once she stepped out of the bathroom, however, she began making excuses for herself, using the dubious reasoning of an addict facing a bender: "I figured as long as I'd stepped over the line, I might as well go all out," she remembers. So she did. She bought more cocaine from a dealer at the nightclub and then stayed out all night with a girlfriend. The next day, Drew took a credit card from Jaid's purse and ran away with her friend. "We both had this fantasy about going as far away as possible, some place like Hawaii, with nothing but the drugs and the credit card," Drew explains.

They purchased two tickets to Hawaii for the following day, then flew to Los Angeles, where they snorted more cocaine and alternated between crashing at Drew's house and driving around town in Jaid's BMW. And then Drew smashed into two cars while attempting to parallel park. "At that point I was so miserable that I actually entertained the idea of driving straight to the hospital. I wanted to. I realized that I was on a crash course with disaster," she reveals in her autobiography.

Instead, Drew and her friend went shopping. By that time, Jaid had reported her stolen credit card and was on her way home from New York. Somehow Drew conned most of the salespeople she encountered and purchased several hundred dollars' worth of clothes with the invalid card. Back at Drew's place, the girls continued to snort cocaine while they packed for Hawaii. Suddenly, two strangers walked in through the unlocked front door.

"Who the [hell] are you?" Drew demanded as one of the strangers approached her, pulling a pair of handcuffs out of a pocket. "I'm a friend," the woman replied, handcuffing Drew's hands behind her back. The "friends" turned out to be private agents hired by Jaid to drag Drew back to ASAP. Relieved that she was not headed for jail, Drew sat in the car silently while the agents badgered the frightened girl with questions about her movies, "which I thought was sick," Drew declares. "'God, you've just yanked me out of my house with cuffs on,' I thought, 'and now you're asking me what it was like to meet E.T. What jerks.'"

At ASAP, Drew tried to pull herself together. She had barely eaten or slept in days, her hair was dirty and matted, and she was shivering from cold sweats. A nurse began talking to her while acquaintances from her previous stays looked on curiously. When one girl finally asked, "How much sobriety do you have?" Drew was tempted to lie. But she knew that the other patients could see right through any tall tales she might invent. "Twenty minutes," Drew whispered in response. "[Shoot], man," she heard the girl say. "She had it going so good too." Drew glanced at the girl, and she could see the sadness in her eyes.

Drew had a difficult time readjusting to life in rehab. She threw tantrums. She fought overwhelming impulses to hide in her room or sit in a corner all day. Eventually, Drew's therapist forced her to acknowledge her situation by asking her during a group meeting, "Have you hit your bottom?" Cornered, Drew suddenly realized exactly what that phrase meant. In Alcoholics Anonymous and other addiction treatment programs, patients are told that they may "hit bottom," or find themselves at the lowest point in their lives, before they will truly work to pull themselves back up again. "Yes," Drew responded honestly, "Yes, I've hit my bottom."

Betty Wyman appointed herself Drew's in-house manager, restricting Jaid's access and taking over parental responsibilities. "Drew was going out [at night] the first time she was in," Betty states. "She and Jaid were treating this almost as if it were hotel ASAP. But this time her stay wasn't going to be like a guest-spot appearance." This time, Drew's full recovery became the priority.

Gradually, Drew began to recognize how much she actually shared with the other patients. She listened

Jaid and Drew Barrymore attend a party with Italian actress Sophia Loren's son. "She has never been a mother to me in the normal sense," Drew has said of her mother, whom she once described as more of a "best friend" than a parent while Drew was growing up.

carefully during group meetings and finally dared to talk about herself. She gained confidence and began to pinpoint the problems that had led to her addictive behaviors: low self-esteem, depression, troubled relationships with her parents, difficulties with classmates and members of the opposite sex. She was reassured when she discovered that these were the same problems that other patients were struggling to overcome.

Like everybody else in the program, Drew experienced good and bad days. In her first month and a half, she was given ITP—"intensive treatment program," a punishment for bad behavior—a record 15 times. But she began to

JOHN **BARRYMORE** JOAN **CRAWFORD** WALLACE **BEERY**

GRETA **GARBO** LIONEL **BARRYMORE**

A Metro Goldwyn Mayer PICTURE

GRAND HOTEL

Until she was in rehab, Drew had never seen any of her famous relatives' films. She was impressed by her grandfather's performance in Grand Hotel *(above), but says that her father's acting in* High School Confidential! *(facing page) "mesmerized" her.*

recognize why she behaved the way she did. "I wasn't able to articulate it, but looking back, I'd describe that rough period as the reemergence of my conscience. There was right and there was wrong, and I saw which side of the line I was standing on," she later said.

A breakthrough occurred when Drew's grandfather, Jaid's father, died. Drew took the news hard, but she expressed her feelings in a group session. "He was one of the people I loved most in the world," Drew admitted. "But I worried I had missed the chance to let him know how I felt because I was into my teenage bullshit and rotten drug usage." For the first time, Drew was letting herself feel pain without trying to numb or escape the emotion by using drugs. Several days later, during a therapy session,

Drew greeted a new patient with the standard refrain, "Hi, I'm Drew and I'm an addict and I have 51 days sober." But this time, she felt very different about the words she was saying. "And that was it," she recalls. "I knew it was true and something had to be done about it."

Drew turned next to the emotions she had stored up for years about her father. "Once, when I was really little, he spent the night with us," Drew said, "and the next morning he came into my room. I looked up at him and asked, 'Dad?' I was really scared he was going to say no, he was just a friend. But he said, 'Yeah.' I felt so happy thinking he was going to be back in my life. But it never happened." When Drew finally revealed the secret she had told no one—that her father had abused her physically and emotionally—she suddenly realized the truth: *he* was very troubled and she was *not* unloved, unworthy, and alone. Finally, she began to feel good about herself and open up to other people. "I talked my head off. I became close to people. I interacted in games, activities, and started coming out in the open."

As a result of her good behavior, Drew was permitted to attend movies and concerts with other patients and with supervisors. They went to parks, played softball and miniature golf, went bowling, and had cookouts at the beach. It was the first time Drew had ever participated in such "normal" activities. And the point was obvious: life could be fun, even when you were sober. When Drew's counselors discovered that she had never seen any of her father's or grandfather's films, they took her to a video store to rent some. She selected John Barrymore's Oscar-winning movie, *Grand Hotel* (costarring her great-uncle Lionel), and John Barrymore Jr.'s *High School Confidential!*, in which he portrays a young drug pusher. "It was cool seeing everyone's names in the first movie," Drew says. "But I was mesmerized when I saw my Dad."

She hadn't seen her father in seven years, but soon after watching the movie she thought she spied him drinking in a park where she was playing Frisbee with fellow patients. The next day, Drew's mother surprised her by informing her that her father had called Drew's agent and had asked for her.

John was probably trying to contact his daughter to get

money, Jaid warned. Nevertheless, Drew telephoned her dad, hoping that he would be "really nice, you know, the dad I'd always wanted." After an emotional exchange in which Drew told John she loved him and he responded, "I love you, too, daughter," John asked for money, and then he hung up temporarily so he could get high.

In counseling sessions and in her own mind, Drew realized that she had to be honest with herself: "He wasn't a good guy to me," she finally admitted. Eventually, she allowed herself to accept the fact that her father was "gone from my life and will never be there for me again. It's hard, but that's the way it is," she recounted in her autobiography.

With her mother, however, Drew had a long way to go. "The most emotional part of my treatment has involved trying to get my relationship with my mother straight," Drew conceded shortly before her release from ASAP. Still, when she left the hospital on December 21, 1988, three months and one week after she had arrived in handcuffs, Drew kissed her mother as she climbed into the car beside her. She felt happy to be on her way home.

Drew had 96 days sober. She was 25 pounds lighter than when she entered rehab, she looked fantastic and felt great, and she was proud of herself and hopeful about her future. But as Drew later explained in her autobiography, "The temptation in recovery is to believe that once rehab is finished, you will be completely healed. The reality, as I found, is quite the opposite. The truth is that you are never fully mended. You just learn how to deal with the problems that intensify your disease."

For Drew, more problems lay ahead.

Drew Barrymore, shown here in a 1989 publicity photo for the ABC television special 15 and Getting Straight, *had just emerged from rehab herself a few weeks before filming began.*

6

LITTLE GIRL FOUND

SHORTLY BEFORE HER discharge from ASAP, Drew found out that the tabloids had discovered she was in a drug rehab center. Whether or not she wanted her personal problems made public, Drew was about to be forced into the limelight once more as America's favorite child star—and a child addict in recovery.

Drew was furious at first, and then she felt helpless and depressed. She had planned some day to speak publicly about what she had experienced as a substance abuser and rehab patient, but she wanted to wait until the time was right for *her.* Unfortunately, the *National Enquirer* made that decision for her. On January 3, 1989, the tabloid announced the lurid news: "*E.T.* Star in Cocaine & Booze Clinic—at 13! The Shocking Untold Story."

Instead of allowing the unwanted publicity to make her feel ashamed and humiliated, Drew devised a plan. Before leaving ASAP, she decided to tell her story in her own words to *People* magazine. If fans were going to hear about her drug use, Drew decided, they should at least hear an accurate account. "Sometimes it's better not to respond to gossip," she says:

> However, I decided that this wasn't one of those times. I think it took courage on my part. But I didn't want to be considered another Hollywood tragedy. That's the last thing I am. I'm a success. That's why I decided to tell my story. If I've learned anything, it's [that it is] always better to tell the truth. And by doing so, maybe it will help other kids not to end up like me.

Her interview appeared in the January 16 issue of *People*. Photographs of Drew at the rehab clinic highlighted a long, first-person account of her struggle with drug abuse. In the article, Drew comes across as realistic and honest; she concludes, "I'm not psychic. But for today I can stay sober. I never want to go back to my old ways. I know that. That is my future. One day at a time. I'm Drew, and I'm an addict-alcoholic. I've been sober for three months, two weeks, and five days, and I'm really proud of that."

During the period of intense publicity that followed, Drew answered hundreds of phone calls, and reporters stalked her house. But she did not allow the media scrutiny to intimidate her; instead, she jumped right back in front of the camera. She had agreed to appear in an ABC After-school Special entitled *15 and Getting Straight*, which began filming a few weeks after her release from ASAP. The movie, which focused on a group of teens in recovery and costarred Tatum O'Neal, Ryan's daughter, was filmed at the same rehab facility where Drew received treatment.

Drew pored over stacks of letters from sympathetic and troubled fans who had heard about her ordeal. "Without question the response made me feel as if I'd done the right thing by going public," Drew determined. "Not getting help would've been something to be ashamed of. . . . There's absolutely no shame in helping other people," she declared.

With the aid of Todd Gold, the journalist from *People*

magazine who had interviewed her, Drew began to transform her journal and writing assignments from her days in rehab into an autobiography. She continued to attend therapy sessions and weekly meetings of Alcoholics Anonymous (AA), and she felt extremely proud of her accomplishment as she approached the benchmark of six full months of sobriety.

And then, as Drew later explained, "I blew it."

Drew's friend Andie was a "bubbly party girl a few years older" who had her own car and was "wild, one of the things that made her so fun," as Drew says in her autobiography. One night the two girls smoked some of Andie's marijuana. "For no good reason other than that. We had the pot and decided to get high," Drew recounts.

It was the night before what would have been Drew's six-month anniversary of getting straight. After an hour of laughing and enjoying her high, Drew began to reflect on what she had just done. She knew that part of her motivation to stay clean came from a desire to prove to everyone "who seemed to be holding my every move under a microscope that I could stay sober. That I wasn't a drug addict." Yet Drew realized that she had also "truly enjoyed" being straight. "I liked feeling healthy and natural and in control. I liked knowing myself, being comfortable with myself, knowing how to deal with problems rather than hiding from them." Suddenly, Drew felt horrible about blowing off all those days of sobriety just for this brief high.

Moments later, Andie's car was slammed by another car traveling in the opposite direction that had crossed over the center line of the road. Drew's head hit the windshield and she was knocked out, but both girls escaped serious injury. Upon reviving, Drew's only concern, she admitted later, was that her slipup in smoking pot not be discovered. Her guilt about breaking sobriety and lying about it dampened the joy she felt over the next two months as she continued to work hard in therapy and at AA.

Then she slipped again—with Andie, who once again

Drew with costars Stephanie Nichols (center) and Tatum O'Neal (right) in 15 and Getting Straight. *Forced by the media to discuss her drug problems publicly, the 14-year-old bravely admitted that she had been in a drug treatment program, but added, "If I've learned anything, it's [that it is] always better to tell the truth. And by doing so, maybe it will help other kids not to end up like me."*

had some pot. Drew's guilt mounted, along with her fear. She felt too embarrassed and too afraid to tell anyone about her lapses, not even her mother or her closest confidante, Jan Dance, a former addict who had become Drew's AA sponsor. "I found I could talk with Jan about anything. Guys, the hospital, my mom," Drew says. "I also listened to her. She'd been through what I was going through, and that counted for a lot." But Drew could not summon the courage to tell Jan that she had failed at staying sober.

Drew began losing the emotional stamina required to

either stay sober or keep deceiving people when she slipped. "I could accept just fine that I'd gotten stoned and broken my sobriety, but I found it too hard, almost impossible, to handle that I couldn't be honest about it and accept the consequences for my actions." Her life slid downhill quickly. She began to fight with her mother and with her boyfriend Peter, a 22-year-old actor. It annoyed her that Jaid had befriended Peter, and she felt doubly abandoned. After running away from home one morning, Drew telephoned Jan Dance's husband, the rock musician David Crosby. A former addict himself, Crosby had become a surrogate father to Drew, and he often provided a sympathetic ear and ready, helpful advice. Wearing his pajamas, David fetched Drew and drove her back to his house for breakfast and some fatherly counsel.

In the spring of 1989, Drew moved into a tiny apartment in West Hollywood with a girlfriend. She was 14 years old. Friends had helped her get a job as a doorperson at several nightclubs, where she worked three nights a week. Looking back, Drew could see that she was not really sober, just dry. "When you're dry," she told *People* magazine the following year, "you don't have the chemicals, but you're doing the same old patterns as when you're loaded. When somebody puts a joint in front of your face, it's easy to say, 'okay.'"

Drew sunk into depression. She gained 10 pounds. She fought with her roommate, and her lies haunted her constantly. When her father telephoned one afternoon in early July, Drew was on the verge of a breakdown. "Though I wasn't even considering using alcohol or drugs to blot out my troubles, I saw myself quickly sinking into a dark abyss," she later recalled of that time.

As usual, her father asked for money. Drew said no, then suffered through a night of remorse. She still longed for a relationship with her father, and she was feeling desperately lonely. "I hated myself. I felt ugly, fat, and useless. I started going crazy. I felt as if I was hexed,"

Jaid Barrymore and her young boyfriend attending a nightclub. One of the biggest steps Drew Barrymore had to take on her road to recovery from substance abuse was coming to terms with the troublesome relationship she had with her mother.

Drew recalls in her autobiography. The next afternoon she got high again with Andie. The following day her mother announced that she was going to New York for a few days—with Peter, Drew's ex-boyfriend.

"All of a sudden everything in my life seemed to be piling up," Drew remembers. She phoned her therapists, but none of them was available. It was the Fourth of July holiday, and Drew was alone, spiraling out of control.

"I ran into the kitchen and could not stop crying. If a gun was there, you know, I might have shot myself, I don't know. I grabbed a knife, and I thought, 'Well, what shows the most pain?'" She slashed her wrist with the kitchen knife and passed out. Fortunately, Drew's roommate, who had come home with a boyfriend, rushed Drew to a nearby emergency room. At her request, Drew was transferred to ASAP, and she reentered the rehab facility for her third and final stay.

This time, the transition to life in rehab was not as difficult for Drew. This time, she really *wanted* to be there. "ASAP represented safety to me. I felt comfortable, secure, like I had come home—not to be coddled, but to be healed," she says. And this time, Drew resolved to face the truth. "No more lies. 'This time do it for you, Drew,' I chanted over and over to myself while falling asleep. 'Be true. Be strong. Do this for yourself.'" She approached Betty Wyman. "We have to do something about my mother," she explained, finally willing to pinpoint the source of her ongoing difficulties.

ASAP persuaded Jaid to check into an inpatient treatment program for "codependents," the loved ones of addicts who unknowingly foster and enable the person's addiction. For Drew to receive the help she needed to permanently overcome her self-destructive behavior, Jaid would have to learn how to maintain a healthy relationship with her daughter. "I come from a very dysfunctional family," Jaid confessed after her codependency treatment. "I grew up in a violent household with lots of anger, so my frame of reference for a solid family structure didn't exist."

Jaid had mostly ignored the signs of her daughter's addictions, overlooking the cigarette smoking and the drunkenness. She instead opted for the opportunity to escort her celebrity child to the Hollywood parties and nightclubs where Drew's addictions got started and were fed for years. Jaid checked into The Meadows, a rehab facility in Arizona, but she promptly checked out again at the end of her first day. She felt incarcerated and she resented the intensity of the program. But Drew quickly set her mother straight.

"You know what?" she told her mother over the phone. "I'm going to tell you something, and it's going to be short and simple. I'm fourteen years old. I've spent seven months of my life in this hospital, working damn hard to get better. You've spent six hours in a hospital. How dare you do that when you say I'm important to you? This is important to us. Stop being so goddamn selfish."

Jaid spent the next six weeks at The Meadows, where she learned exactly how she had failed to be a good parent to her child. In the meantime, Drew worked on the same issue at ASAP. She eventually concluded, "She has never been a mother to me in the normal sense and it was silly to try to create that relationship. We've always been more like best friends, I decided, and truth be told, I really did miss her friendship."

So when Drew was ready to leave ASAP in October after 45 days, Betty Wyman determined that Drew would be better off in a different environment. This time, she went home with David Crosby and Jan Dance. "I knew her father back when I was using [drugs]," David Crosby told *People* magazine a few months after Drew moved into his ranch house in the San Fernando Valley. "I felt she had been dealt a short deck, you know, a fifth-generation alcoholic, and I didn't want to see her go down the tubes."

The rock guitarist who headed Crosby, Stills, Nash, & Young in the 1970s had recovered from a 25-year pattern of heroin and other drug addictions. He went solo professionally, wrote a popular autobiography, and lived a successfully sober life. Not only was Crosby an excellent role model for Drew, but he was also the first strong paternal figure in her home life. "I would not presume to try and supplant her parents," Crosby said. "But she needed to be around some people that were committed to

Rock star David Crosby (shown here) and his wife, Jan Dance, who are recovered addicts themselves, became surrogate parents for Drew in the difficult period following her release from ASAP.

sobriety, and God knows, Jan and I are. We put a lot of energy into staying straight." So did Drew. And this time, living in a more conventional family environment, she succeeded.

Drew accepted the Crosbys' rules, adjusting to their strict curfews and scheduled mealtimes. She reveled in their friendship and guidance. As time passed, she discovered that her need for constant attention from boys diminished. "Basically, what I was looking for in men or boys was acceptance. You want to feel pretty, you want to feel loved, you want to be hugged, you want to feel adored. . . . And sometimes that gets out of control. It certainly did with me." Crosby's loving presence filled the void created by Drew's troubled, unavailable father.

Drew Barrymore, fully recovered, in 1990. "Some people have this image that when you get clean, you become this perfect angel, and it's really not like that," she said the year she turned 15. "You don't lose the urge to be naughty. You just learn to gain control over it."

While living with the Crosbys, Drew made new friends (most of whom were former drug abusers like herself) and stayed away from clubs and bars. She cleaned her room and did her own laundry. She worked on her autobiography and she turned 15. And Drew stayed sober, an achievement that she viewed from the mature perspective of a recovered addict: "Some people have this image that when you get clean, you become this perfect angel, and it's really not like that," she said. "You don't lose the urge to be naughty. You just learn to gain control over it." In a March 1990 interview, she admitted that "the scariest question I've been asked is 'Are you going to stay sober for the rest of your life?' because I have no control over that. I have no idea. I can only take it one day at a time."

So she did. And she stayed out of trouble, while evolving into a person whom she herself enjoyed being around. The little girl who had grown up too fast now found that she enjoyed being a child again in an environment where she was encouraged to be her very best self. "To tell the truth, I used to be really in the dark about why all this stuff was happening to me," the 15-year-old said about her five years of substance abuse. "But . . . I'm a believer in fate. . . . As weird as it sounds, I wouldn't change anything that happened because I really like where I am today, and if I didn't do what I did for the last five years I wouldn't have these things."

Drew went for long rides on her horse, a brown beauty named Mocha Baily. She flirted with bronzed surfers on the beaches of Hawaii while David Crosby watched in amusement. And she dreamed about returning to work, about landing a really good part in a really great film. Finally, Drew Barrymore felt like she could be herself—and act her age. "You know, when you become sober, you don't own a halo," Drew declares. "You've just got to do the best that you can."

Drew as a waitress named Julia in the 1998 film The Wedding Singer.

7

EVER AFTER

A FEW WEEKS after its release, Drew's captivating, sometimes shocking autobiography, *Little Girl Lost,* climbed to the top of the best-seller lists. Not content to settle for a number one slot as an author, Drew longed for a film role that would put her back in the spotlight she truly loved: on the movie sets of Hollywood. She did not have to wait long before this dream came true.

But first, Drew decided that she needed to get her home life in order. She did this by divorcing her parents. Resorting to California's Emancipation of Minors Law, Drew carried out the same legal steps her character, Casey Brodsky, took on-screen in the 1984 film *Irreconcilable Differences*. The procedure absolves parents of all responsibility and liability for their children but does not declare them incompetent (a legal term that would brand them as unqualified to be adequate parents). In Drew's case, the judge decided in favor of emancipation.

Drew was now legally free to marry, receive medical care, and establish credit or residency without parental consent. She was also legally able to work the same number of hours as adults. She had difficulty paying the rent, so she took a temporary job in a coffee shop. But what Drew needed was a job she could do well—one in front of a movie camera. By this time, Drew had officially dropped out of school, and she began to focus all of her energy on reviving her acting career. "It is," she said at the time, "my pride and joy."

It was difficult, however, to convince major studio executives that a 15-year-old former addict was the right person for *any* role. After taking a few minor parts in several forgettable films, Drew landed a hefty role on a hip new CBS television show, *2000 Malibu Road*. The summer series became a cult hit in 1992; its loyal audience enjoyed the show's weird California characters and artfully distorted camera angles. "Everything about the series seemed enlarged, heightened, wonder-drugged," reflected the *New Yorker* in the fall of 1992. Drew, who played an innocent young woman trying to make it in Hollywood, also earned good reviews: "Everything she did in *2000 Malibu Road* was belly-button playful. . . . the camera forgives her everything," one reviewer enthused.

Drew was so well received in her next three movies that by 1993, *Cosmopolitan* magazine had anointed her "possibly the best, and certainly the most daring, young actress of the nineties." As the dangerously sexy Ivy in *Poison Ivy*, Drew made a career comeback, seducing movie audiences along with most of the other characters in the film.

Drew enjoyed playing the role of the campy seductress. "I knew this movie was going to do exactly what I wanted it to do for me," she explained later. "I wanted something crazy that no one would expect of me."

The Amy Fisher Story was one of three competing TV movies about a lurid true story in which a 16-year-old shot her lover's wife in a jealous rage. Drew skillfully played the lead role in the ABC version. Although all

Sporting dark tresses, Drew (bottom center) made a comeback in the 1992 TV series 2000 Malibu Road.

three programs were disparaged by many people, who decried the fact that the accused teen, her lover, and his family profited from the publicity, *Time* magazine called Drew's performance "sulky, smoldering."

Drew defended her decision to take the Amy Fisher role as part of her attempt to create a startling new image for herself. This is why Drew also decided to do *Guncrazy*, which she calls one of her two favorite film roles (the other is Gertie in *E.T. The Extra-Terrestrial*). In *Guncrazy*, Drew played another likable but trashy character, Anita, a lonely high schooler who lives in a trailer park and begins corresponding with a prison inmate. After her pen pal is freed, he marries her and takes her on a "romantic" Bonnie and Clyde–style killing spree. Although it premiered on

As Anita, a lonely high school girl who becomes involved with a convict (played by James LeGros, right) in Guncrazy, *Drew Barrymore welcomed the opportunity to create a new screen image for herself.* Guncrazy *was one of her two favorite film projects. The other?* E.T. The Extra-Terrestrial.

television, *Guncrazy* attracted such a huge fan following that the film was also released in theaters. The eminent movie critic Vincent Canby wrote in the *New York Times*: "Drew Barrymore gives the kind of performance that can transform a sweetly competent actress into a major screen personality." Which was, of course, Drew's plan for herself all along.

During 1992 and 1993, Drew starred in seven movies in addition to the short-lived *2000 Malibu Road*. She was building a reputation as a bankable professional actress who could handle challenging and daring roles. No longer a child star or Hollywood wild child, Drew Barrymore was evolving into a leading lady. It was a reputation she could be proud of.

In person, Drew seems tiny, more petite than she appears on-screen. When she was 18, she described her weight-control and beauty methods for *Cosmopolitan* magazine. Dressed comfortably in ripped jeans, a dungaree jacket, and combat boots, Drew wore no makeup and little jewelry. "I'm so embarrassed," she laughed, "because honestly, my beauty regimen is: I don't work out, and all I eat is really bad junk food, and, um, sometimes I like good food too. . . . When I was younger, I had a really bad weight problem. I looked like a damn butterball, couldn't even get a job because I was so fat." She continued:

> I didn't know anything about good eating. I studied nutrition. . . . And I would work out every day for two hours. I did that for eight months, lost forty pounds, and I had the most incredible body by the time I was done. . . . I was so proud of myself that I had actually accomplished this.
>
> It was difficult after that, because anything I ate, I would immediately gain the weight back. . . . And then, all of a sudden, one day . . . I really wanted to eat my favorite food, macaroni and cheese. . . . And I just said, "I'm gonna eat and I don't care what happens. I'm just tired of living my life feeling guilty about every single bite of food I put in my mouth." And ever since then—it's been three and a half years—I've pretty much eaten whatever I wanted and remained the same weight.

Her fans certainly appreciated Drew's natural, feminine, and voluptuous figure, but they also recognized her great acting talent. She had become an icon—an object of adulation and envy. As a model for Guess? jeans, Drew was indeed a nineties-style pinup girl, posing carefully so that the colorful flash of her tattoos made up for the absence of a shirt.

Her most devoted fans already knew about the butterflies, the cross with rose vines on her ankle, and the cherub on her back with the illegible name of a lover who became her fiancé—and her ex-fiancé—in 1993. Jamie

Walters, the *Beverly Hills 90210* actor, had posed with Drew for a magazine cover before their breakup, Drew hiding some of her nude body (and her tattoos) behind her boyfriend's fully clothed pose. Drew, who regards nakedness as more of an expression of freedom than sexuality, was enjoying herself—still sober, but still wild.

On March 20, 1994, Drew impulsively married her boyfriend of six weeks, a 31-year-old Los Angeles resident and Welsh-born bar owner named Jeremy Thomas. The unorthodox ceremony took place around 5 A.M. in The Room, Thomas's dimly lit bar on Cahuenga Boulevard in Hollywood, with a minister they found listed in the local Yellow Pages. Drew borrowed a cream-colored satin slip dress from one of the bartenders. Thomas slipped a diamond and gold band that had belonged to his grandmother and then his mother on his bride's finger. Following the strawberry cheesecake and the champagne toast—"I wanted to have a sip of champagne at my wedding, and that's what I had," Drew admitted afterward—the dial-a-minister, who also worked as a professional psychic, informed the couple that they had known one another before, "in a previous life." Drew was impressed, "because that's exactly how I feel. Everything about us is like fate," she told *People* magazine less than a month after the ceremony.

Just a few hours after the impromptu wedding, the new bride flew to Tucson, Arizona, where she was still in the midst of filming *Boys on the Side*, a *Thelma and Louise*–style movie starring Whoopi Goldberg, Mary-Louise Parker, and Drew as a lovable waitress who's on the run after accidentally killing her abusive boyfriend. This was Drew's second "chick flick," on the heels of the popular cowgirl movie *Bad Girls*, in which she costarred as a Wild West hooker alongside Madeleine Stowe, Mary Stuart Masterson, and Andie MacDowell.

Boys on the Side proved to be a big success, but Drew and Jeremy's marriage did not. A few weeks after the couple's delayed honeymoon trip to Santa Barbara, *People*

Drew Barrymore and former boyfriend, Beverly Hills 90210 *actor Jamie Walters, in 1993.*

magazine reported rumors of Drew's "change of heart" and her plans to file for divorce. By the time *Boys on the Side* was released in 1995, the marriage was over and Drew was feeling bitter.

"He needed the marriage, and I stupidly agreed to it," Drew said of the union that she now attributes to Thomas's quest for a green card (an ID card that allows a foreign-born person to have permanent resident status in the United States). In marrying, Drew helped him to become an American citizen. But she was also in love, while he was mostly interested in his own future. "It was such a joke. The whole thing was a [stupid] lie. The

Director Woody Allen (right) gives advice to Edward Norton and Drew Barrymore on the set of the 1996 musical comedy Everyone Says I Love You. *One movie reviewer later called Drew a "delightful presence" in the film.*

press lied about it, we lied about it. . . . It's really ruined marriage for me," Drew lamented after her divorce.

In addition to her scene-stealing performance in *Boys on the Side,* Drew landed two other roles in 1995. In *Mad Love,* Drew plays Casey, a willful and spontaneous high school girl who wins Chris O'Donnell's devotion even after he learns that she is mentally ill. "The story is so innocent, it's beautiful," the actress told *Rolling Stone* magazine. In a later interview, she discussed the emotional difficulties of playing a manic-depressive and suicidal teen. "I became this girl so much, and in order to pull it off, it took so much from me. But in the end, it was very worthwhile," she said.

As a change of pace, Drew appeared with Val Kilmer, Jim Carrey, and Chris O'Donnell in *Batman Forever*, playing Sugar, the frilly henchwoman for Tommy Lee Jones's evil character, Two-Face. Drew styled her bleached-blond character as a tribute to one of her Hollywood idols, Marilyn Monroe. The film's director, Joel Schumacher, who had directed her in *2000 Malibu Road*, gushed, "There was no Sugar on the face of this earth except Drew Barrymore. She is cotton candy with marshmallow breath."

Drew also headed the trendy cast of the hip 1996 horror film *Scream* before beginning work on Woody Allen's musical comedy *Everyone Says I Love You*. As Skylar, a demure prep-school character, Drew sings a duet (her voice was dubbed) with Edward Norton, who plays her character's fiancé. "She is a delightful presence throughout the film, bringing an untypical air of toothsome innocence to the part," said the *New Statesman* of Drew. During filming, Drew became fond of costar Goldie Hawn and of Woody Allen, whom she called "my favorite friend in the whole world." After filming ended, Drew shared an apartment with another new friend, Edward Norton, in her new favorite place, the West Village in New York City.

By this time, Hollywood had begun offering Drew Barrymore the kind of roles that allowed her to play characters much like herself—a good woman who insists on seeing the good in others. In doing so, she had moved up the Hollywood ladder from being a B-movie slasher-vixen to being a talented romantic lead actress. And her own life was developing a joyfully romantic story line as well.

After breaking up with the rock guitarist Eric Erlandson, the 21-year-old actress fell in love again. In an interview with *Harper's Bazaar* in 1996, Drew revealed that she hoped one day to move to Texas with her unnamed

Drew Barrymore's warm-hearted nature is well-known both in Hollywood circles and among her fans. Here, she helps to decorate a Volkswagen Beetle during a fund-raising effort for pediatric AIDS patients in 1997.

boyfriend, where they would build a farm and start a family. Her secret beau turned out to be Luke Wilson, whom she met on the set of *Best Men*, a small film still seeking American distribution. The two worked together again in *Home Fries* (1998), in which Drew plays a pregnant fast-food worker. Although Drew and Luke parted ways in December 1998, they remain close and see one another as often as they can.

Since the breakup, Drew has spent her time getting acquainted with herself. "Sometimes it's strange, because I don't have love in my life—in the boyfriend sense," she told *Teen People* in May 1999. "But I have it from other places, and hopefully, always from myself. I no longer have the fear of being alone. . . . It's cool to find out that you don't need a boyfriend to be happy." Despite Drew's professed willingness to go it alone, however, some media sources have more recently linked her with *Saving Private Ryan* star Jeremy Davies.

The exciting success of her own film company makes Drew glowingly happy. She established Flower Films in 1994 as a means of shaping the films she really wants to star in—and see. She firmly believes that experiencing pain and hardship can transform one into a more sympathetic, spiritual person, and that's what she aims to portray in the movies she produces. "As an actor I'll want to continue to do darker characters," she told *InStyle* magazine in March 1999, "but the only movies I want to produce for people are fun, caper[-like], funny, romance movies—all the good stuff in life." Her friend Edward Norton concurs: "Drew has a more sincere instinct for giving than anyone of our generation I've met in this business. She has forged this terrific positivity out of life."

Today, watching *Melrose Place* is Drew's only addiction; she has every episode taped and sent to her when she is away from home. She also loves to watch *Jeopardy,* and calls game show host Alex Trebek "a hotty." A plate of macaroni and cheese makes Drew very happy, as do her dogs, yellow mutts Flossie and Templeton. She reads voraciously, keeps a journal, and still considers herself a nerd. Her worst habit is twirling her hair around her fingers.

Drew's body makes her happy, too, although she now claims, "I'm not going to take my clothes off anymore. I don't do wild things anymore." As for her continued reputation as a sex kitten, Drew laughs, "I've never looked in the mirror and said, 'You look hot!' But it's important to feel good about yourself. . . . I finally realized I don't have to have an A-plus perfect body, and now I'm very happy the way I am."

The way she is includes keeping herself happy by helping other people feel good. For example, while on location in an isolated village in France shooting *Ever After* (1998), the well-received feminist version of the Cinderella fairy tale, the thoughtful actress endeared herself to her crew by supplementing the set's skimpy supply of catered food with vegetarian sandwiches and fresh fruit. Offscreen, Drew doesn't eat meat, fish, or eggs; nor does she wear shoes made from leather or other animal by-products. She also raises funds for Wildlife Waystation, a rescue organization for wild animals, because she believes that animals deserve to be happy, too.

When she purchased her own home, a solar-heated, recycled-cedar barn in Coldwater Canyon in the Los Angeles hills, Drew invited her homeless father, John Barrymore Jr., to move into an apartment over her garage. "It's weird because we've never lived together," Drew told *Mademoiselle* in 1998. "We're actually really close now," she stated in another interview, "which is nice. He started wearing shoes and I stopped wearing shoes—kind of ironic."

But Drew is no longer close to her mother. When she was 20, Drew got back in touch with Jaid after more than four years of silence, but mother and daughter remain distant, and Drew is somewhat unhappy about a situation she is unable to change. "I don't understand her. And I tried to for so long," Drew says of Jaid, who has pulled such coattail-riding stunts as taking bit parts in Drew's films and posing for *Playboy* eight months after her daughter had.

"I just think that too much [stuff] has happened," Drew says vaguely when asked why she refuses to see her mother. Drew never puts her mother down, but explains, "I think we differ in the fact that she seems to love Hollywood and I hate Hollywood. . . . It's a shallow, inconsistent, competitive, cruel world. Whenever I get really sad that I'm involved in it, I feel that instead of sitting on the sidelines and complaining, I should go in there and make it better. I like making movies, so I want to make good movies. . . . And as a producer, I want to create a great working atmosphere for people, and I know how to do that. It's in my blood and in my bones."

This may explain why Drew has taken to producing and starring in the types of movies that make viewers feel good. "Upsetting movies scratch my psyche the wrong way," she told *Time* magazine after appearing in the goofy romantic comedy *The Wedding Singer* (1998) with former *Saturday Night Live* regular Adam Sandler. "I want to laugh and escape and see love and romance. That's where I'm at."

Drew is taking her happiness one day at a time—"I'm definitely one of those cosmic, out-in-the-ether, chickie dudes," she says of her happy-face attitude and hippie-style optimism. But she is also a living testament to the power of self-healing. She is an inspiration to anyone who has struggled to overcome the trauma of a difficult, abusive childhood, and a role model for those who understand the psychological strength and spiritual integrity required to overcome addiction. In more than two decades before the camera, Drew has acted in more than 30 films. And she has changed right before our eyes, continually reinventing herself to become one of the most popular and admired actresses of her generation. She has become the person she once dreamed of being.

Drew Barrymore is beautiful, bubbly proof that apple dumplings, too, can take on Hollywood and, ever so sweetly, transform a life-shattering curse into a happy blessing to share with the world. "Endings should be surprising," she says, paraphrasing the famous novelist Flannery O'Connor, "but inevitable."

CHRONOLOGY

1975 Drew Barrymore born on February 22 in Culver City, California, after her parents, John Barrymore Jr. and Ildyko Jaid Mako, separate

1976 Appears in first TV commercial

1978 Appears in first TV movie, *Suddenly, Love*

1980 Appears in first feature film, *Altered States*

1982 Costars in *E.T. The Extra-Terrestrial* and becomes a celebrity at seven years old

1983 Receives British Academy of Film and Television Arts Award of Best Outstanding Newcomer for role in *E.T. The Extra-Terrestrial*

1984 Films *Irreconcilable Differences* and *Firestarter*; begins drinking alcohol and smoking cigarettes

1985 Appears in *Cat's Eye*

1986 Appears in TV movie *Babes in Toyland;* tries marijuana; has first thoughts of suicide

1988 Begins using cocaine; briefly enters drug rehab facility and reenters for 3½ months

1989 Appears in *See You in the Morning* and *Far from Home*; moves into her own apartment; returns to rehab following relapse and suicide attempt; moves in with David Crosby and Jan Dance

1990 Publishes best-selling autobiography, *Little Girl Lost*; obtains legal divorce from parents; stars in TV program *15 and Getting Straight*

1992 Appears in TV series *2000 Malibu Road;* stars in *Poison Ivy* and *Guncrazy*

1993 Stars in TV movie *The Amy Fisher Story;* nominated for Golden Globe Award for role in *Guncrazy*

1994 Costars in *Bad Girls*; marries Jeremy Thomas (they divorce after 51 days); cofounds Flower Films production company

1995 Costars in *Boys on the Side* and *Mad Love*; appears in *Batman Forever*

1996 Appears in *Scream*

1997 Costars in Woody Allen's *Everyone Says I Love You*; Flower Films signs two-year deal with Fox 2000

1998 Stars in *The Wedding Singer, Ever After,* and *Home Fries*

1999 Produces and stars in her own first film, *Never Been Kissed;* is nominated for an American Comedy Award and Blockbuster Entertainment Award for role in *The Wedding Singer;* is nominated for Blockbuster Entertainment Award for *Ever After*

2000 Produces and appears in *Charlie's Angels: The Movie;* narrates *Titan A.E.*

2003 Starred in and produced the sequel to *Charlie's Angels, Charlie's Angels: Full Throttle*

FILMOGRAPHY

Suddenly, Love (TV movie, 1978)

Altered States (1980)

Bogie (TV movie, 1980)

E.T. The Extra-Terrestrial (1982)

Firestarter (1984)

Irreconcilable Differences (1984)

The Adventures of Conn Sawyer and Hucklemary Finn (TV movie, 1985)

Cat's Eye (1985)

Babes in Toyland (TV movie, 1986)

The Ray Bradbury Theater (TV episode, 1986)

The Screaming Woman (TV movie, 1986)

Conspiracy of Love (TV movie, 1987)

Far From Home (1989)

See You in the Morning (1989)

15 and Getting Straight (TV special, 1990)

The Dennis Miller Show (TV episode, 1992)

Guncrazy (1992)

Motorama (1992)

No Place to Hide (1992)

Poison Ivy (1992)

Sketch Artist (TV movie, 1992)

2000 Malibu Road (TV series, 1992)

Waxwork 2: Lost in Time (1992)

The Amy Fisher Story (TV movie, 1993)

Doppleganger: The Evil Within (1993)

Wayne's World 2 (1993)

Bad Girls (1994)

Inside the Goldmine (1994)

Batman Forever (1995)

Boys on the Side (1995)

Mad Love (1995)

Everyone Says I Love You (1996)

Like a Lady (1996)

Scream (1996)

All She Wanted (producer/actress, 1997)

Best Men (unreleased in U.S., 1997)

Wishful Thinking (1997)

The Barrymores: Hollywood's Royal Family (TV special, 1998)

Ever After (1998)

Home Fries (1998)

The Larry Sanders Show (TV episode, 1998)

Ruby Wax Meets (TV episode, 1998)

The Wedding Singer (1998)

Never Been Kissed (producer/actress, 1999)

Scream 3 (producer, 1999)

Charlie's Angels: The Movie (producer/actress, 2000)

Titan A.E. (voice only, 2000)

Riding in Cars with Boys (2001)

Freddy Got Fingered (2001)

Donnie Darko (2001)

Confessions of a Dangerous Mind (2003)

Duplex (2003)

Charlie's Angels: Full Throttle (2003)

FURTHER READING

Barrymore, Diana, with Gerold Frank. *Too Much, Too Soon*. New York: Henry Holt, 1957.

Barrymore, Drew, with Todd Gold. *Little Girl Lost*. New York: Simon & Schuster, 1990.

Barrymore, Ethel. *Memories: An Autobiography*. New York: Harper & Brothers, 1955.

Barrymore, John. *Confessions of an Actor*. Indianapolis, Ind.: Bobbs-Merrill, 1926.

Barrymore, Lionel, with Cameron Shipp. *We Barrymores*. New York: Appleton-Century-Crofts, 1951.

Berlin, Joey. *Toxic Fame: Celebrities Speak on Stardom*. Detroit: Visible Ink Press, 1996.

Brooks, Amy. "Never Been Better." *Teen People,* May 1999.

Cawley, Janet. "The Barrymore Curse: Can Drew Beat It?" *Biography*, April 1998.

Crosby, David. *Long Time Gone: The Autobiography of David Crosby*. New York: Doubleday and Company, 1988.

Drew, John Jr. *My Years on the Stage*. New York: Dutton, 1922.

Drew, Louisa Lane. *Autobiographical Sketch of Mrs. John Drew*. New York: Charles Scribner's Sons, 1899.

Kotsilibas-Davis, James. *The Barrymores: The Royal Family in Hollywood*. New York: Crown Publishers, 1981.

Millea, Holly. "Drew's Rules." *Premiere*, September 1998.

Peters, Margot. *The House of Barrymore*. New York: Alfred A. Knopf, 1990.

Rohrer, Trish Deitch. "True Drew." *InStyle,* March 1999.

Schneller, Johanna. "Happily Ever After." *US*, November 1998.

APPENDIX

WHERE TO GET HELP FOR SUBSTANCE ABUSE

Drew Barrymore is one of thousands of people who have overcome drug abuse and addiction. The following list includes agencies, organizations, and websites where you can find information on drugs of abuse. You can also learn where to go for help with a drug or related problem.

Many national organizations have local chapters listed in your phone book. Look under "Drug Abuse and Addiction" to find resources in your area.

Alcoholics Anonymous
P.O. Box 459
Grand Central Station
New York, NY 10163
212-870-3400

American Council for Drug Education
164 West 74th Street
New York, NY 10023
212-758-8060
800-488-DRUG (3784)
http://www.acde.org/

Center for Substance Abuse Treatment
11426-28 Rockville Pike, Suite 410
Rockville, MD 20852
800-662-HELP (4357)

Children of Alcoholics Foundation, Inc.
555 Madison Avenue, 4th Floor
New York, NY 10022
212-754-0656
800-359-COAF (2623)

Cocaine Anonymous
6125 Washington Boulevard, Suite 202
Culver City, CA 90232
800-347-8998

Cocaine Hotline
800-COCAINE (262-2463)

D.A.R.E. (Drug Abuse Resistance Education) for Kids
http://www.dare-america.com/
index2.htm

Drugs Anonymous
P.O. Box 473
Ansonia Station, NY 10023
212-874-0700

Hazelden Foundation
http://www.hazelden.org/

Just Say No International
2000 Franklin Street, Suite 400
Oakland, CA 94612
800-258-2766

Narcotics Anonymous
P.O. Box 9999
Van Nuys, CA 91409
818-773-9999

National Adolescent Suicide Hotline
800-621-4000

National Clearinghouse for Alcohol and Drug Information (NCADI)
P.O. Box 2345
Rockville, MD 20847-2345
800-729-6686
800-487-4889 TDD
800-HI-WALLY (449-2559, Children's Line)
http://www.health.org/

National Institute on Drug Abuse (NIDA) Hotline
800-662-HELP (4357)

National Substance Abuse Hotline
800-HELP-III (435-7444)

Parents' Resource Institute for Education (PRIDE)
3610 DeKalb Technology Parkway, Suite 105
Atlanta, GA 30340
770-458-9900
http://www.prideusa.org/

Students Against Destructive Decisions (SADD; formerly Students Against Driving Drunk)
Box 800
Marlboro, MA 01750
508-481-3568

Students to Offset Peer Pressure (STOPP)
P.O. Box 103, Dept. S.
Hudson, NH 03051-0103

Youth to Youth
700 Bryden Road
Columbus, OH 43215
614-224-4506

FIND OUT MORE ABOUT SUBSTANCE ABUSE AND ADDICTION

Aronson, Virginia. *How to Say No*. Philadelphia: Chelsea House Publishers, 2000.

Center for Substance Abuse Prevention (CSAP). "Tips for Teens About Alcohol." National Clearinghouse for Alcohol and Drug Information (NCADI) Publication #PHD323. Rockville, Md.: CSAP, 1996.

—————. "Tips for Teens About Crack and Cocaine." NCADI Publication #PHD640. Rockville, Md.: CSAP, 1996.

—————. "Tips for Teens About Hallucinogens." NCADI Publication #PHD642. Rockville, Md.: CSAP, 1996.

—————. "Tips for Teens About Marijuana." NCADI Publication #PHD641. Rockville, Md.: CSAP, 1996.

Connolly, Beth. *Through a Glass Darkly: The Psychological Effects of Marijuana and Hashish*. Philadelphia: Chelsea House Publishers, 1999.

De Angelis, Gina. *Nicotine and Cigarettes*. Philadelphia: Chelsea House Publishers, 2000.

Harvard School of Public Health. "A Guide for Teens: Does Your Friend Have an Alcohol or Other Drug Problem? What You Can Do to Help." NCADI Publication #PHD688. Boston: Harvard School of Public Health, 1994.

Hasday, Judy, and Therese De Angelis. *Marijuana*. Philadelphia: Chelsea House Publishers, 2000.

Holmes, Ann. *Psychological Effects of Cocaine and Crack Addiction*. Philadelphia: Chelsea House Publishers, 1999.

Kozar, Richard. *How to Get Help*. Philadelphia: Chelsea House Publishers, 2000.

Kuhn, Cynthia, Scott Swartzwelder, and Wilkie Wilson. *Buzzed: The Straight Facts About the Most Used and Abused Drugs from Alcohol to Ecstasy*. New York: W. W. Norton and Company, 1998.

McFarland, Rhoda. *Drugs and Your Parents*. New York: Rosen Publishing Group, 1997.

Mothers Against Drunk Driving (MADD). "Some Myths About Alcohol." http://www.madd.org/UNDER21/youth_myths.shtml. Irving, Tex.: MADD, 1998.

National Clearinghouse for Alcohol and Drug Information (NCADI), Center for Substance Abuse Prevention. *Drugs of Abuse.* NCADI Publication #RP0926. Rockville, Md.: NCADI, 1998.

——— . *Straight Facts About Drugs and Alcohol.* Rockville, Md.: NCADI, 1998.

National Institute on Drug Abuse (NIDA). "How Not to Get High, Get Stupid, Get AIDS: A Guide to Partying." NCADI Publication #PHD622. Bethesda, Md.: NIDA, 1993.

Peacock, Nancy. *Drowning Our Sorrows: Psychological Effects of Alcohol Abuse.* Philadelphia: Chelsea House Publishers, 1999.

Somdahl, Gary L. *Drugs and Kids: How Parents Can Keep Them Apart.* Salem, Oreg.: Dimi Press, 1996.

INDEX

Alcoholics Anonymous
  (AA), 83, 84
Allen, Woody, 101
Altered States, 46
Amy Fisher Story, The
  (TV movie), 94-95
Arch Street Theater, 27
ASAP Family Treatment
  Center, 69-72, 73-79, 81,
  86-87

Babes in Toyland
  (TV movie), 64
Bad Girls, 98
Barrymore, Blythe, 40
Barrymore, Dede (Dolores
  Ethel), 34, 38
Barrymore, Diana (aunt),
  18, 32, 34, 37-38, 51
Barrymore, Drew Blyth
  appearance of, 13, 15,
    68-69, 97, 103
  autobiography of, 12, 13,
    16-17, 18, 45, 46, 48, 52,
    56, 59, 62, 71, 72, 73,
    79, 82-83, 86-87, 90, 93
  birth of, 43
  and charities, 104
  childhood of, 12, 13-17,
    41, 44-53, 55-65
  and cigarette smoking,
    16, 61, 62, 87
  and decision to become
    actress, 46
  and divorce from parents,
    55, 93-94
  and drug and alcohol
    addiction, 11, 13, 15,
    16-17, 22, 41, 58, 62-64,
    67, 68-79, 81-91

and early acting career,
    45, 46-51
  education of, 49-50, 52,
    56, 58, 59-60, 64, 94
  family of, 14-15, 17-18,
    25-41, 51-52, 65
  fans of, 21-22, 27, 82
  film production company
    of, 12, 19-20, 103
  home of, 104
  and marriage, 12, 21,
    98-100
  as movie producer, 12, 105
  and party scene, 58-59,
    61-65, 72-73
  personality of, 13, 20-23,
    41, 60-61, 65, 97-98, 105
  relationships of, 20,
    97-98, 101-103
  and suicide attempt, 12,
    86-87
  and treatment for drug
    and alcohol addiction,
    69-72, 73-79, 81, 82,
    83, 87-91
  TV appearances of, 52
Barrymore, Ethel (great-
  aunt), 18, 25, 27-28, 29,
  30, 31, 32, 34-35
Barrymore family, 14-15, 17-
  18, 25-41, 51-52, 65, 78
Barrymore, Georgie (great-
  grandmother), 27, 28
Barrymore, John (grand-
  father), 18, 25-26, 27-30,
  29, 30-36, 38, 76, 78
Barrymore, John Drew
  (father), 15, 17-18, 34,
  38, 43-44, 45-46, 53,
  78-79, 85, 104

Barrymore, John III, 39, 41
Barrymore, John Jr. (John
  Blyth) (father). *See* Barry-
  more, John Drew
Barrymore, Lionel (great-
  uncle), 18, 25, 27-28, 29,
  30, 31, 32, 34-35
Barrymore, Maurice (great-
  grandfather), 27, 28, 29
Batman Forever, 22, 101
Beau Brummel, 33
Big Night, The, 38
Blyth, Herbert. *See* Barry-
  more, Maurice
Bogie (TV movie), 47
Boys on the Side, 98-99,
  100

Cal Prep, 64
Canby, Vincent, 96
Cat's Eye, 16, 59
Churchill, Winston, 29
Colt, Ethel ("Sister"), 36
Colt, John Drew ("Jackie"),
  36
Colt, Russell, 31
Colt, Samuel Griswold
  ("Sammy"), 36
Costello, Dolores, 33-34,
  35-36, 38
Country School, 58
Crosby, David, 85, 88-90,
  91
Cukor, George, 26-27, 34,
  36, 52

Dance, Jan, 84, 88, 89-90
Davies, Jeremy, 103
Dinner at Eight, 35
Drew, John, 27, 29

Drew, Louisa Lane
  (Mummum), 27, 28, 29

Erlandson, Eric, 20, 101
E.T. The Extra-Terrestrial,
  11, 13, 48-51, 52, 55, 95
Ever After, 13, 104
Everyone Says I Love You,
  22, 101

Far from Home, 68, 71
Fenwick, Irene, 32
Fields, W. C., 35
15 and Getting Straight
  (TV special), 82
Firestarter, 16, 56, 59
Flower Films, 12, 19-20, 103
Floyd, Mamie, 28
Fountain Day School, 50, 52
Fox 2000, 19-20

Gish, Lillian, 52
Gold, Todd, 82-83
Grand Hotel, 78
Guncrazy, 95-96

Hamlet, 32
Harris, Katherine, 31
Hawn, Goldie, 101
High School Confidential!,
  38-39, 78
Home Fries, 102

Irreconcilable Differences,
  55-56, 58, 93

Jacobs, Elaine, 36
Justice, 32

Juvonen, Nancy, 19

King, Stephen, 16, 56, 57, 59

Little Girl Lost (autobiography), 12, 13, 82-83,
  90, 93

Mad Love, 100-101
Madonna, 20
Mako, Ildyko Jaid (mother),
  boyfriend of, 85, 86
  childhood of, 43
  and divorce, 43-44
  and Drew's acting career,
    45, 46, 55, 67, 68, 71
  and Drew's addiction, 69,
    71, 74, 86, 87-88
  as Drew's escort to
    parties, 69, 71, 74, 86,
    87-88
  Drew's relationship with,
    15, 61-62, 65, 69, 74,
    85, 87-88, 104
  and Drew's relationship
    with father, 78-79
  homes of, 44, 56
  and marriage to John
    Barrymore, 43-44, 46
  in rehab facility, 87-88
  as waitress and actress,
    14, 43-44, 46, 104
Meadows, The, 87-88
Miglietta, John Drew, 36

Never Been Kissed
  (producer/actress), 20
Nightingale, The, 31

Norton, Edward, 22, 101,
  103

Oelrichs, Blanche, 32, 33, 34
O'Neal, Ryan, 55-56

Palazzoli, Gabriella, 40
Poison Ivy, 13, 94

Rasputin and the Empress,
  34

Saturday Night Live, 52
Schumacher, Joel, 101
Scream, 101
Sea Beast, The, 33
See You in the Morning,
  67-68
Spielberg, Steven, 11, 16,
  48, 49
Suddenly, Love (TV movie),
  45

Thomas, Jeremy
  (ex-husband), 98-100
Tonight Show, The, 52
2000 Malibu Road
  (TV series), 94, 96

Walters, Jamie, 20, 97-98
Ward, Jennifer, 57, 59
Wedding Singer, The, 13, 105
Westland, 56
Wildlife Waystation, 104
Williams, Cara, 39
Wilson, Luke, 20, 102
Wyman, Betty, 69, 74, 87,
  88

PICTURE CREDITS

page

2: Corbis
10: Reuters/Jeff Christensen/ Archive Photos
14: Reuters/HO/Archive Photos
17: Corbis
19: AP/Wide World Photos
21: AP/Wide World Photos
24: Corbis
26: Archive Photos
30: AP/Wide World Photos
34: Photofest
37: Photofest
39: Corbis
40: Photofest
42: AP/Wide World Photos
44: Photofest

47: Corbis
49: Photofest
50: Photofest
54: AP/Wide World Photos
57: Photofest
58: Photofest
60: Darlene Hammond/ Archive Photos
62: Corbis
67: AP/Wide World Photos
68: Photofest
70: Ron Wolfson/London Features
75: Nick Elgar/London Features
76: Photofest
77: Photofest

80: AP/Wide World Photos
84: Photofest
86: Corbis
89: Photofest
90: Gregg De Guire/ London Features
92: Photofest
95: Photofest
96: Photofest
99: Archive Photos
100: Photofest
102: Ron Wolfson/London Features
107: Nick Elgar/London Features

Virginia Aronson is the author of more than 17 books, including health textbooks, self-help guides, and biographies for young readers. She has written several titles for Chelsea House, among them *How to Say No, Venus Williams,* and *Ann Landers and Abigail Van Buren.* She lives in South Florida with her writer husband and their young son.

James Scott Brady serves on the board of trustees with the Center to Prevent Handgun Violence and is the vice chairman of the Brain Injury Foundation. Mr. Brady served as assistant to the President and White House press secretary under President Ronald Reagan. He was severely injured in an assassination attempt on the president, but remained the White House press secretary until the end of the administration. Since leaving the White House, Mr. Brady has lobbied for stronger gun laws. In November 1993, President Bill Clinton signed the Brady Bill, a national law requiring a waiting period on handgun purchases and a background check on buyers.